"When Jesus called the original disciples, He said, "follow me." That is essentially what it means to be a disciple of Christ. We are Christ followers today because they took the challenge. In turn, they challenged others. Now it is our turn. This book will not only help you be a disciple, but will also equip you to lead others to take the challenge. Clarence is one of my beloved disciples."

—GARY CHAPMAN, Ph.D. author of *The Five Love Languages*

"Clarence Shuler beautifully brings all facets of discipleship to life in this workbook. He gives the faith-based community its very own manual to navigate through this ever-challenging journey called *life*. Read this book and keep it on your nightstand!"

—MONICA WRIGHT, WNBA Player and WNBPA Executive Committee, 2-Time WNBA Champion, Minnesota Lynxs, First Team All American, University of Virginia

"Discipleship is key to discovering *what* you believe and *why* you believe it. *The Challenge*, has done the "heavy lifting" of the *how*. Dr. Shuler's strategy has the right balance of scholarly insight and practical application that both the new convert and the mature yet undiscipled believer can employ for a healthy walk of faith. . . .

Organized, comprehensive, meaningful examples, and effective exercises. True to his proven endearing style, Shuler takes a "walk with" approach making this guide easy to follow as if it were seemingly custom-crafted for each participant."

—STEVE FITZHUGH, Certified NFL Engagement Coach, NFL Player Engagement

"I've read some excellent books describing what discipleship is but I've never seen anything as practical as this one. Clarence literally shows you how to be discipled and how to disciple others. *The Challenge* is an excellent hands-on resource for passing on our devotion to Jesus Christ."

—DR. JULI SLATTERY. Psychologist, President and Co-Founder of Authentic Intimacy

"Clarence has written a powerful guide that will help unlock the great potential God placed in us through the key of discipleship."

—ANDREW POWELL, Southern Colorado FCA Area Director, former Air Force Academy football player

"This book by Dr. Shuler is a fundamental, thorough guide on how to strengthen your walk with Jesus. Years of tried-and-true knowledge come together in an engaging manner of faith and action. 'What's up, Doc; you've done it again!'"

—ADRIAN BRANCH, ESPN College Basketball Analyst, NBA Champion, 1987 Los Angeles Lakers

"*The Challenge* is not only a must-read, it is a must-do. Clarence Shuler guides readers through the powerful principles of discipleship succinctly and pragmatically. This book will change lives!"

—LEAH GREEN, ESQ., Attorney at Law, author of *No Trespassing: I'm God's Property*

"Clarence Shuler has been studying and teaching the topic of discipleship for decades. The Challenge is the result of that study, providing Christ-followers young and old with practical steps, to mature in their own relationship with God, and to lead others in pursuit of Him."

—GREGG HUNTER, President/CEO, Christian Camp and Conference Association

"Dr. Shuler has developed a methodical disciple-making workbook that will inspire readers to pursue God's Great Commission. He has provided all the tools necessary and supporting Scripture for one-on-one and group settings. Outlined five-day action plans in various sections facilitate group discussions and understanding of the subject matter. I personally have used multiple books to achieve the same results but with this well-crafted workbook, I will be able to purge more than just a few books from my library."

—NATE ATKINS, Calvary Worship Center; Safety Director, former Los Angeles Police Officer, former member of The Navigators

"*The Challenge* invites us back to the priority of discipleship in a very transparent way. What my friend Clarence has modeled through his life, he now makes available through his pen—practical and insightful teaching of God's Word. Get ready to absorb and apply."

—DR. JOHNNY PARKER, Author of *Turn the Page: Unlocking the Story Within You,* Former Life Coach for the Washington Redskins

"Dr. Shuler chooses a good title for his book with the word, "Challenge." Of all the things people are being challenged to do today we need to be challenged to help others grow to maturity in Christ. As the author says the one of the biggest indicators that someone is a disciple of Jesus Christ, is that they have helped someone else become a disciple of Jesus. *The Challenge* offers the reader scores of practical tools to help know what to do in helping another person grow to maturity in Christ. I recommend this book for anyone who wants a better grasp of disciplemaking and the practical tools needed for the journey."

—EDDIE BROUSSARD, International Vice President, The Navigators

"Clarence Shuler has done a great job in making discipleship practical and hands on. Pastors and church leaders need a book like this to take members through stages of growth in a systematic way. Discipleship covers more than just Bible knowledge but a life change. The Challenge is packed with Scripture references that provide a backdrop for the steps on discipleship. Shuler has given the church a treasure chest of verses that are helpful in defining a disciple of Christ. I recommend The Challenge to all who desire to grow deep in Christ."

—RICH BERRY, The Navigators

The Challenge

Cultivating Disciples That Last

Building Lasting Relationships Publishing House
Colorado Springs, Colorado

The Challenge: Cultivating Disciples That Last © 2018 by Dr. Clarence Shuler

Editor: Briana Pringle & Amy Roemer
Cover Illustrator: Bev Cotton
Interior Designer: Glynese Northam

ISBN-13: 978-1546356905

Library of Congress CN: 2017907025

Contact Dr. Clarence Shuler (a.k.a. "The Love Doctor"):
E-mail: Clarence.BLR@gmail.com
Website: www.clarenceshuler.com
Facebook Community Page: Building Lasting Relationships
Twitter: @clarenceshuler

The Challenge

Cultivating Disciples That Last

with Leader's Guide and Prayer Journal

CLARENCE SHULER

TABLE OF CONTENTS

DEDICATION

To my wife, Brenda, you encouraged me to write this. Our daughters, Christina, Michelle, and Andrea, you motivate me to do much of what I do!

To Jean, thanks Sis. You're a special inspiration and blessing to me, and I'm grateful you field-tested this. Thanks to your children, too, Jonathan and Jennifer Blakney.

And to my brother, Junior Brown, I love you.

ACKNOWLEDGMENTS

Gary and Karolyn Chapman

As the guides who served my coming into relationship with Jesus Christ, I'm forever grateful to God for you. I'll always remember how you taught and encouraged me to memorize God's Word. You've invested your lives in mine—and in my family's. (Shelley and Derek, thanks for sharing your dad with me.) Investing in others, helping them, and then watching those persons grow in faith in Christ—you all have been teaching *discipleship* to many. I'm so grateful for your efforts!

God said we are to "entrust" what we've learned to others (see 2 Timothy 2:2). Gary, you've shown me, "You haven't made a disciple until your disciple makes a disciple." Making disciples has always been a challenge, but always worth the effort. Thanks for helping me help others grow.

Robert and Jean Cook

For 23 years, Bob, you mentored and invested in me in so many ways! Thank you. Your sponsoring this workbook is typical of you. I wish you could have seen it completed. But you're in His presence now. I'll never forget how much you loved and protected Jean. You were so gracious to share your life, time, and resources with me.

Gordon and Beth Loux

Thank you, both! Gordon, I'm grateful for your affirmation, encouragement and wisdom.

Dr. William and Hazel Pannell

Thank you for sharing your gifts of insight and critical thinking God has given you.

To those individuals across this country who allowed me to *disciple them*, given me *spiritual grandbabies*, and to those who have *taught me about discipleship* through their lifestyle, thank you. There's not enough I can say, but I've tried to share in the additional acknowledgments.

Briana Pringle, thank you for your editorial service on this book. Bev Cotton, thank you for your incredible illustrated cover. *Glynese Northam*, thank you for your beautiful interior design work. Thank you, for this wonderful teamwork on this project as a labor of love for Jesus Christ!

To those individuals across this country who allowed me to *disciple them*, given me *spiritual grandbabies*, and to those who have *taught me about discipleship* through their lifestyle.

It is also dedicated to the late Dr. *Mark Corts*, his son, Dr. *Stephen Corts*, Executive Pastor *Olus & Nikita Holder*, Pastor *LeRon & Marlene West*, *Don & Shelley Kentner*, Associate Worship Pastor *John* & Global Missions Director *Ronda Tyson, Bill & Vickie Markham*, Rev. *James & Marian Jones, Stan & Debbie Senft, Travis Jones, Dwight & Barbara Morrison*, Bishop Dr. *Courtney* & Pastor *Janeen McBath, Gary & Jean Jennings, Ferrell & Trese Foster, Bill Weedman*, Pastors *Ben & Wanda Anderson* of Solid Rock Church, Pastor *Don & Lurlie Sharp* of Faith Tabernacle Baptist Church, Associate Worship Pastor *Richie Kingsmore* of Calvary Baptist Church, *Robert & Kay Watson, Doug & Linda Hill, Derek & Tricia Crews, Phil & Donna Pepperl, Gerrit & Celeste Wolfaardt, Keith & Beverly Jemison, Bill (Butch)* & the late *Rushella Latimer,* the late *Matthew* & late *Viola Daniels, Sr.,* and the late *Willard & Elreno O'Neal.* And to all my spiritual family in Tulsa, Oklahoma: Drs. *John & Shelley McGirt, Davy & Elliott McGirt, Derek & Amy Chapman, Brian & Ginny Teel,* Calvary Revival Church, Lighthouse Covenant Fellowship, Dr. *Bob & June Ewell, Al & Susan Mueller,* Pastor *Cedrick Brown,* Family Pastor *Gary Warren, Ed & Becky Householder, Craig Glass,* the late *Dallas & Opal Schafer, Bill* & the late *Harriet Briggeman, Rich & Jane Berry, John* & the late *Betty Bass, David Guy,* Pastor *Jerald & Maura January* & the late *Jerra January, Andy* & the late *Arlene Elcock, Tom & Sydna Masse,* Dr. *Johnny & Lezlyn Parker, Andrew & Samantha Powell, Scott & Jess Shuford, Vince & Cindy D'Acchioli, Al & Angela Caligone, Tim & Ina Meyer,* Dr. *Sam & Linda Huddleston,* Pastor *John & Trina Jenkins,* Dr. *Willie Richardson, Phillip Lane, Chuck Allor, Darryl & Deborah Colbert, Monica Wright, Shahid Wilds, Doug Nichols, Don Nicholson, Roger Banner, Mark & Teri Holombo, Sam & Dara Ritter.* To all my

Prayer Partners around the world, and Calvary Baptist Church of Winston-Salem, NC.

Thanks to my pastor, *Al Pittman, Norma*, his wife and Calvary Worship Center.

To *Michael Jones*, former Chairman of the Board of Directors of *BLR: Building Lasting Relationships* and to *Steve Wamberg* again for his initial assistance with this workbook's Leader's Guide. And to my other faithful Board of Directors, *Donna Scott, Rodger & Gloria Henn, Vernard Gant, Jennifer Oraker-Holtz*, and *Brenda* for their wisdom and patience with me.

Thanks to James Bellanca for taking BLR to the next level redesigning the website and putting all the free videos on it.

Thanks *Jerry & Judy Kelow* and *Todd & Lisa McLain* for providing tremendous assistance for this workbook by going through this course, finding errors and making suggestions to improve this workbook.

Thank you, *Amy Roemer*, for working so closely with me while editing this workbook.

I'm incredibly grateful to *Barry & Lawanna St. Clair* of Reach Out Youth Solutions for their friendship and prayers. They graciously allowed me to use some of their materials in my sessions in section one, Lordship, growing deeper roots and keeping time.

Thank to my brothers on The Fatherood Commision Board, *Stephen Kendricks* (The Kendrick Brothers, Inc.), *Bill Eyster*, Chairman of this board, *Brian Blomberg*, Development Officer for New Life Ministries, *Brian Doyle*, President of Iron Sharpens Iron, *Jeff Kemp*, TeamKemp and author of THE BLITZ, and *Mitch Temple*, Executive Director.

The Challenge: Who, What, How

Jesus Christ defines *discipleship* as:

➤ us
➤ denying ourselves,
➤ taking up our crosses daily, and
➤ following Him.

Jesus affirms losing our lives for His sake (Luke 9:23–25). Discipleship is a serious challenge. We need God's hand on us, and one another's help during this lifelong process.

The Challenge encourages changed lives that have an impact through growth. This doesn't require us to forfeit life; being disciples in Christ means gaining real life for ourselves and helping others find the same joy. Going forward in life this way brings the greatest joy we can experience. It's biblical; it's blessed (see Psalm 1).

The biblical principles in *The Challenge* help answer questions for those who are curious about Christ, and help those seeking to gain *more* in their life with Christ; more understanding, increased intimacy with God, and increasing influence for Him. Some participants in *The Challenge* will gain that relationship with Him. Others, who know Jesus personally, will find that this study nurtures new spiritual growth. This book encourages all of us to draw closer to Christ, offering discipleship growth paths and ongoing strategies for increasing our impact. Every participant in *The Challenge* can grow and cultivate a lifestyle of seeking God, and helping others.

Every follower of Christ can make disciples. As Jesus' first followers increased in wisdom and understanding, and then multiplied in numbers, our challenge today is to continue that cycle (Matthew 28:18–20). Jesus spent three years investing His life to nurture 12 men to follow Him, as well as the extraordinary group of women who not only followed His lead, but also helped to sustain His ministry (Luke 8:1–4). And they continued to grow.

Then and now, becoming a *disciple* involves learning, but also includes relationship, and increasing service to others that has a lasting impact. This involves that *change*, and brings fruitfulness. Change is usually challenging because we're moving out of our comfort zones, which requires faith as well as discipline. The rewards will be great.

> *"I appointed you so that you might go and bear fruit—fruit that will last—and so that whatever you ask in my name the Father will give you. This is my command: Love each other" (John 15:15–16 NLT).*

WHO AND WHAT

We have not made a disciple until *our* disciple makes a disciple, which makes us spiritual grandparents! *The Challenge* teaches Christ followers about investing in themselves spiritually—and in others who will follow Christ: "The things which you have heard from me in the presence of many witnesses, entrust these to faithful men *who will be able to teach others also*" (2 Timothy 2:2; emphasis author's). This study has goals for each of us:

➤ Mature spiritually in a personal relationship with Jesus Christ.
➤ Develop mutually beneficial relationships with other disciples.
➤ Consider disciple-making a lasting lifestyle.
➤ Find fulfillment for life by serving, and helping others grow.

Through independent as well as group gatherings, this study provides for:
➤ Increasing dependency on Jesus Christ alone.
➤ Maintaining a consistent time alone with Jesus.
➤ Developing Christ-like qualities, biblical priorities, and quality relationships.
➤ Improving service to people in diverse and inclusive ways.
➤ Sharing one's faith story with confidence and competency.
➤ Teaching, modeling, and other disciple-making practices.
➤ Using time, talent, and all of life to help point others to God.

The Challenge has specific criteria:
➤ Develop and maintain consistent devotional time with Jesus.
➤ Focus on God through worship, prayer, reading Scripture; meditating on and memorizing Scripture daily.

➤ Complete preparation sections.
➤ Attend *Challenge* sessions regularly.
➤ Fellowship with your group.
➤ Trust in the process.
➤ Seek opportunities to serve others in community.
➤ Continue to participate in small-group or related class(es).
➤ Support and invest time in a local ministry or church through prayer, financial help, and other giving.

HOW

Join *The Challenge*. Anyone who desires to grow spiritually and obey Christ's command of making disciples, or any person on a spiritual journey, seeking Christ, can participate in this individual and group experience.

WHEN AND WHERE

You can record here your *Challenge* group's time and meeting place.
Starts (place and date): _____
Completion (place and date): _____
Scheduled Day: _____
Scheduled Time: _____

Those who choose to join *The Challenge*, please provide this information to the group leader(s), along with a signature:
Name: _____
Address: _____
Phone: _____ email: _____
City: _____ State: _____ Zip Code: _____
My Signature: _____ Date: _____

FRUIT THAT WILL LAST

Discipleship is the biblical and best way to live a life that has lasting impact in this world and eternity. This is about more than numbers, although we do see what happens when individuals multiply outreach for Christ (you can see this in the chart).

17

Jesus came to reconcile us with God and to *transform* our lives. Studying God's Word and gathering with others in church are only a part of the transformational process. *Discipling* is about a personal and spiritual transformation that can't be kept from overflowing into the lives of those who cross our paths. The Bible describes this as *fruitfulness*.

The Challenge emphasizes this personal interaction through *life-on-life* experiences. Biblical discipleship is biblical *knowledge* and interpersonal *relationship*; not *either or* but *both and*.

Gary Chapman began to disciple me when I was a 17-year-old. He introduced me to Christ when I was 16 years old, helped me to grow in Christ, became a father figure for me, and is a lifelong friend. That help—his hand in my life—changed me forever! Like Gary and me, fellow disciples gain relationship, discover more of life's purpose and their destiny, and together fulfill the Great Commission (Matthew 28:18–20). As His followers, we disciple others; we reproduce, increase (John 15:8).

Chart Year	Addition People	Multiplication People
1	365	2
2	730	4
3	1,095	8
4	1,460	16
5	1,825	32
6	2,190	64
7	2,555	128
8	2,920	256
9	3,285	512
10	3,650	1,024
11	4,015	2,048
12	4,380	4,096
13	**4,745**	**8,192**
33	**12,045**	**8,589,934,592**

8.5+ billion people, challenges the world population of 7.4 billion (estimated March 2016). Discipleship makes sense.

18

Without question, leading a group of disciple-makers through *The Challenge* is one of the most exciting experiences in my life because I watch many leaders and participants see their lives change. Nurturing disciples that last is a spiritual journey with immediate and eternal consequences!

BEFORE WE GET STARTED

As we engage the biblical principles in *The Challenge*, you may encounter some principles new to you, or that give you a different perspective. Ask God to reveal to you what is true through *His Word*. Use a notebook or computer to record your questions, insights, and answers.

When preparing for your group sessions with this book, you'll connect with the most important book that consists of the Old and New Testament Scripture. The Bible will demonstrate *truth* rather than *opinion*. If there is a teaching that you feel contradicts the teachings of your pastoral leaders, please inquire with your leaders, one or more of them, to gain any clarification.

May God continue to bless you and your family richly as you study and apply His Word to your life, as you follow Christ.

Clarence

JOSHUA 1:8–9

SESSIONS OVERVIEW

These sessions engage participants on multiple levels:

➤ *Individual study and meditation:* daily, for about 30-minutes. *The Challenge* in each session of this book provides five days of activities for participants to do on your own.

➤ *Small-group interaction:* Each *Challenge* small-group session revolves around these group activities:

➤ *Helping Hands:* This begins group time with engaging questions and activities. And also provides opportunity for follow-up and review of previous session content and on-your-own activities. This provides encouragement for participants to share with one another.

➤ *Growing Together:* Bible study and discussion centers on what God's Word says and how we respond.

19

➤ *Cultivating Our Spirit:* This time allows *God's* hand to touch our hearts and minds through the power of His Holy Spirit. It includes sharing memory verses, prayer requests, and introduction to next sessions.

➤ *Bearing Fruit:* This allows check-in on participants' personal exposure to and application of the biblical principles studied in daily segments (completed between group sessions), allowing individuals to dig deeper into Scripture, encourage each other to learn memory verse(s), and focus on principles related to session topics. These are times for practical sharing and discipleship within community. We'll share about the challenges we have on our own, and in connection with others.

Now let's dig into the first group session. Here's information on getting acquainted with others and preparing for success in Part 1 of *The Challenge.*

PART 1 GETTING TO KNOW JESUS

MEETING JESUS

CULTIVATING OUR
SPIRITUAL PASSION

UNDERSTANDING
THE HOLY SPIRIT

PRAYER—
TALKING
WITH GOD

*T*o begin the process of becoming a Christian community – a "safe place" that helps us to discuss spiritual issues, receive support, and gain encouragement as we experience discipleship—let's get to know each other.

In this first session, the group will go through introductions and become familiar with one another. Each participant will tell:

➤ "My lifestyle and how I use my time;
➤ A favorite hobby or interest I have or what I would like to do if I had time to do it;
➤ One fact people may be surprised to know about me; and
➤ Where I see myself on my spiritual journey or how long I have been a Christ follower."

GROUP DIRECTORY

Please help to complete your group's directory by providing your contact information. Your group leader or facilitator will give his or her information first. You can write yours here:

Name	Cell Phone	Email

HELPING HANDS

During this time, you'll be prepared to share answers to questions your group facilitator will ask. Your facilitator will respond first, followed by each group member.

GROWING TOGETHER

FAITH STORY

In the first group session, we'll also take time to talk about how each of us can come to faith in Christ—and what's "our story"—where we might be on our spiritual journey. Apostle Paul tells about his journey to faith in Christ in the Book of Acts. When forming into one of two groups, which your group leader will facilitate, each subgroup will choose one of the following Scripture passages to discuss (subgroups each will report findings to the whole *Challenge* group)

- Acts 22:1–22,
- Acts 26:1–23.

Subgroups will read their passage and then discuss questions 1–4. You'll want to prepare for that discussion.

1. How would you briefly summarize the events that took place in the passage you read?
2. What was Paul's life like before his personal encounter with Jesus?
3. How would you describe what happened to Paul?
4. How did Paul change after his encounter with Jesus?
5. How are these two accounts about Paul similar, yet different (Acts 22:1–22 and 26:1–23)?

Your group will choose a spokesperson to share about these thoughts.

CULTIVATING OUR SPIRIT—MY FAITH STORY

These questions will help you to develop your faith story:

1. Before encountering Christ, what was my life like?
2. How did God "get my attention?"
3. How did I respond?
4. How has my life changed since I entered into a personal relationship with Jesus Christ?
5. If I don't have a personal relationship with Jesus Christ, where am I on my spiritual journey?
6. Am I where I want to be?
   Why? Why not?

BEARING FRUIT

Each week this section will help further personal growth in Christ. It's personal preparation work before each interactive session with the group facilitator and the other disciples in each group. To get the most out of *The Challenge*, complete this section beforehand. This is an opportunity to grow in faith by making a personal application. This includes prayertime alone and with the group, and other spiritual disciplines and activities.

Doing this will require discipline. It's part of *The Challenge*—it will be worthwhile to schedule it! And to pray for others' growth.

If there is ever a time when you feel overwhelmed and don't complete your personal study before the next group gathering, come anyway; *you are more important than the material.*

Your group consists of people who will love and miss you if you aren't part of *The Challenge* group sessions. You are part of this community. Also, feel free to reach out and connect with one or more of the others in your small group as you get to know one another.

JOURNALING OPPORTUNITY
What I Want to Remember: write it in your book, on the back pages of this book, or in a separate journal or computer. You'll want to journal to record your growth.

Meeting Jesus

OUR OBJECTIVE:
Learning first what a *Christian* (Christ follower) is; to have assurance of salvation in Jesus Christ (a personal relationship with Christ); and learning how to share a faith story about Jesus Christ to help others.

OUR MEMORY VERSES: Romans 6:23; 10:9–10 (optional: John 5:24)

DAY 1

Gain a better understanding of who the Father of Jesus Christ is, and how He feels about us. Yes, *Jesus loves us.* In order to understand God's salvation—His rescue of us—we must try to comprehend His *love* for us.

➤ Read 1 John 4:19.
Did we love God first or did He love us first? (Write response here or feel free to use your personal journal.)

➤ Read Genesis 1:26–28.
What does God do for us?

What do these verses tell us about how God feels about us?

Why do I think God feels this way about me?

Did I do anything to earn or make God feel this way about me?

It's critical for us to begin with God's love for us before attempting to understand His salvation—rescue—of us.

REFLECT: Is this the kind of God I want to follow? If "Yes," why?

DAY 2

Let's discover exactly what is required to be a Christ follower. Today, write your faith story of how you became a follower of Jesus Christ. If you're curious about Jesus Christ, but wouldn't label yourself a follower, write your thoughts about where you are on your spiritual journey and why.

Your personal faith story is one of the most powerful and effective tools you have to tell others about Jesus. If you don't have a personal faith story about your relationship with Jesus Christ, please be prepared to share with your group where you are in your spiritual journey. For example, since you are participating in this group:

➤ What has sparked your curiosity so that you joined this group?

➤ What do you want to learn about Jesus Christ and possibly His followers?

The outline of the faith story can still be helpful to you as well. So please, don't feel you can't participate in this growth opportunity—you are part of this community! To assist you in the process of creating your faith story, the following is a faith story outline and a sample faith story.

FAITH STORY OUTLINE

A faith story is the telling of how you came to a personal relationship with Jesus Christ. It's told for the purpose of establishing the fact and credibility of your life in Christ now, as opposed to your life before and without Jesus Christ.

COMMON CHARACTERISTICS OF A PERSONAL FAITH STORY
➤ Your faith story has authority because it is your personal experience.
➤ Your faith story communicates and relates because it's vital, fresh, and alive.

OUTLINE OF A PERSONAL FAITH STORY
➤ Your life before you met Jesus
➤ Your realization of your need for Christ (what sparked your interest)
➤ Your faith commitment experience—actually asking Christ into your life
➤ Your life since making a personal commitment to Christ

CRITERIA IN PREPARING A PERSONAL FAITH STORY TO SHARE WITH OTHERS
➤ *Keep your faith story short, simple, and to the point* (3-5 minutes). Be sensitive not to abuse the time people give us to share about Christ, or you will turn them off to the Gospel, making it difficult for the next person who witnesses to them. People can always ask to hear more.
➤ *Give adequate detail.*
➤ *Keep it positive.* Avoid bragging and negative statements, and be careful about using names of people in a negative manner. If you are using a name of a person in a positive manner, if possible, get their permission and tell him/her how you will be using his/her name.
➤ *Use language* those who aren't following Christ or attending church can understand.
➤ *Keep fine-tuning, rewriting your faith story, and practice telling your faith*

story. Ask family, friends, and select people from church for their *constructive criticism*. Share your faith story with non-Christians, possibly fellow students, co-workers, and neighbors. Be creative in sharing your faith story with non-Christians. Have them listen and ask them to critique. You can tell them you are doing it for a church or group-related class, which is true. This is a way to share with your non-Christian friends without making them defensive.

SAMPLE FAITH STORY

The following pages include my faith story, as an example to help you to write your own.

Clarence Shuler's faith story

I met Jesus Christ May 8, 1970, at a retreat in Hillsville, Virginia. I knew something about Jesus because my parents made me attend Sunday School and church until I was 14. Naturally, as soon as I had a say in the matter, I stopped going to church.

I met Russell, who was to be my best friend for the next 4 years. Basketball was my god! I was born and bred in North Carolina, where we have basketball, tobacco, and Baptists, pretty much in that order.

Russell went to an "integrated" school and I went to an "all-Black" school. Some of Russell's "white" Christian friends invited him to their church. Their church had just built a gym. Russell didn't want to be the only *Black* in the gym, so he asked me to go with him. I was his 4' 8" bodyguard! I didn't care *who* was going to be there if we were going to play basketball!

These white people were nice, which shocked me because this was in North Carolina in 1968 and racist tension was intense. *Whites* were my enemy!

We played basketball for a while, then everyone sat down and we discussed Christians and dating. With topics like *Sex and the Christian* or *Dating and the Christian*, it wasn't boring! Each week's topic was relevant. Discussions would last one hour; then you could play for another hour. Dr. Gary Chapman, our discussion leader, would then tell us how we could accept Jesus Christ into our hearts as our personal Savior and Lord, by asking Him to forgive us of our sins and to come into our hearts to live.

For the next two years, I don't remember missing a single youth night.

Even though I was popular at school, my family was well off financially (or at least I thought we were), and I had a nice girlfriend, I began seeing that the people in this church had something in their lives that I was missing. For two years, I watched Dr. Gary Chapman's lifestyle. He was the most Christ-like person that I had ever met. He still is!

Being short, racial prejudice, my insecurity, and my parents—seemingly always being on my case—were the primary issues with which I was struggling.

On a youth retreat in Virginia in May of 1970, Gary preached a sermon asking this question: "Is your life complete, or is something missing?" I realized something was missing in my life. I had thought that by making the high school basketball team, all of my needs would be met. They were not! The glory of basketball would always fade away. I needed Jesus Christ in my life.

On May 8, I asked Jesus Christ to forgive me for my sins, to come into my life as my Lord and Savior, and to make my life what He wanted it to be. Gary had shared John 3:16 with me, saying, "God so loved *Clarence*, that He gave His only begotten Son that whosoever believes in Him will not perish, but will have everlasting life."

My life changed dramatically! God gave me an inner peace that stays with me no matter what the situation. He also taught me to accept myself the way I am. I'm learning and enjoying the freedom of being an individual, and He began transforming me into a leader. Most importantly, I began living the wonderful life God had already planned for me before I was even born (Psalm 139:14–16: Ephesians 2:10)!

Now it's your turn! Write your faith story. Don't worry about making it sound like anyone else's. Make it yours. Keep it simple. Try keeping it to one page; two at the most. You'll give your story to your leader at the next group session.

DAY 3

Who is a follower of Christ? Today we'll discover what the Bible says is necessary to become a follower of Jesus Christ.

Some people believe a follower of Christ is someone who:
➤ treats people in a way he/she would like to be treated (basically, a "good person")
➤ does good things for people, community, etc.

➤ goes to church regularly, gives money for church work, sings in the choir, etc.
➤ feels sorry for his or her sins
➤ has been baptized, takes Communion, and celebrates other church rituals
➤ is related to a pastor, missionary, etc.

Criteria for a person becoming a follower of Christ are found in the Bible. Let's see what the Bible says about beginning a personal relationship with Jesus Christ. Find the following verses in the Bible. Please feel free to use the *internet* to search, or use the *table of contents* found in a Bible. The Romans verses listed, often called *"The Romans Road,"* explain how to become a Christ follower.

If you own a print Bible, personalize it with a hi-liter, bookmark, underline, and make notes. Hi-lite the verses in this section with the same color. Then, in the front of your Bible write the phrase "Criteria for becoming a follower of Jesus." Highlight this phrase with the same color hi-liter.

BAGGAGE FROM MY PAST

Express, in your own words, what each of the following verses communicates to you:

- Isaiah 53:6
- Romans 3:10
- Romans 3:23
- Romans 5:12
- Acts 4:12

According to these verses above, what separates people from God?

GOD'S GOOD NEWS FOR US

- Romans 6:23
- Romans 5:8
- Romans 10:9–10
- Ephesians 2:8–9

Scripture shows us why we need to follow Christ and how that happens. *Reliable indicators* reveal that a person has accepted Christ.

DAY 4

The reliable indicators that a person has accepted Jesus Christ into his or her life are also in Scripture. Please read and make notes:

New relationship with Jesus Christ:
- 2 Corinthians 5:17
- Romans 15:13
- Acts 1:8
- Galatians 5:22–23
- 1 Thessalonians 1:6
- 1 Peter 3:15
- 1 John 5:18 (NLT, NASB or NIV)
- 1 John 3:9 (NLT, NASB, NIV, compare with King James Version)

DAY 5

How can I be sure Jesus Christ is in my life?

Now that we know how a person becomes a follower of Christ, some of us still question. Insecurity makes growth difficult. In order to be effective— what the Bible calls *fruitful*—we need to have assurance of our personal relationship with Jesus. This assurance is the springboard for being in the "Body of Christ"—the whole community of those who are *Christian*.

Some people believe they can determine if *someone else* is a follower of Christ by observing what that person *does* or *does not do*. However:

➤ This determination comes only between God and each individual person.

➤ Studying the assurance of relationship with Christ is for the follower of Christ to evaluate his or her life *personally*.

➤ This study is not designed to judge or condemn others' lifestyles.

➤ The *visible* signs, which *seem* to indicate that a person is a believer are motivated hopefully by an *inward* commitment to Jesus Christ.

➤ *Outward* signs are meaningless without an inward commitment. Through faith and grace, God plants in each of us a life of obedience to Him (Ephesians 2:8-9).

➤ The following verses help us answer the question: "How can I be sure I have Jesus Christ in my life?"

Explain these Scriptures in your own words:
- 1 John 2:3–6
- 1 John 3:14
- 1 John 3:23
- 1 John 3:24 & 4:13
- 1 John 5:1
- 1 John 5:3

Finish the following statement, based on the content of the preceding verses: "I can be sure of my personal relationship with Jesus Christ because:

_____

_____

_____

_____

If you're eunsure about whether you have a personal relationship with Jesus Christ, pray, reflecting on the verses you've studied. Recognize that sin (doing your very best, yet falling short of God's standards) separates you from God. Declare that Jesus is Lord, and believe in your heart that God raised Christ from the dead (Romans 10:9). You will receive the *free* gift of salvation. Talk with your group leader or pastor about any questions you have. The truth is what the Bible *tells* us; not what our *feelings* may be.

DEEPER ROOTS, MORE FRUIT

Let's see how we can have confidence as followers of Jesus Christ, according to the following verses. For each verse, write what it communicates to you.

- Isaiah 43:13
- John 10:27–30
- 2 Corinthians 5:5
- Ephesians 1:13–14
- Matthew 28:20b (*b* part is the second part of the verse)

How do you feel after reading these verses? Why? What questions do you have about what you have studied? Be prepared to share with your *Challenge* group.

WHY MEMORIZE GOD'S WORD?

Especially with all the technology at our fingertips? The more we work our brain, the better it responds. Some researchers say most people only use a small percentage of their brain. The brain God created produces all of our technology. Let's use our minds and not waste them! God's Word is beneficial everywhere: in church, at home, work, play—wherever we go. We need to memorize God's Word, storing it in our hearts:

➤ "I have hidden your word in my heart that I might not sin against you" (Psalm 119:11).

➤ "These commandments that I give you today are to be upon your hearts" (Deuteronomy 6:6).

➤ Psalm 19:7–11 lists more benefits of knowing and applying God's Word. Verse ten suggests "eating" the Word: "They (God's Words) are sweeter than honey from the comb."

➤ "As a man or woman thinks, so he or she acts" (Proverbs 23:7).

31

SOME PRACTICAL STEPS FOR MEMORIZING BIBLE VERSES:
READING THE VERSE SEVERAL TIMES ALOUD
➤ Helps in understanding the verse.
➤ Helps with memorizing the verse more quickly because the more senses used increases speed and recall ability. Reading and later quoting the verse aloud also keeps the mind from wandering.
➤ Consider putting the verse or verses for that week on paper notes on a mirror. Read them aloud in the morning and at night before going to sleep.

COMPREHEND THE VERSE
➤ Helps you to use the verse correctly.
➤ Read the passages before and after your memory verse for its *context*.

DIVIDE THE VERSE INTO NATURAL PHRASES
➤ Using pauses or natural breaks in verses makes them easier to memorize.

LEARN THE REFERENCE AS PART OF THE VERSE (CHAPTER AND VERSE)
➤ Learning the reference helps us mentally locate the verse in the Bible.
➤ Helps person with whom we are sharing the verse be able to find it.
➤ Say aloud the reference before and after the verse.

LEARN TO SAY THE VERSE PERFECTLY
➤ It is as easy to learn the correct verse rather than memorizing it incorrectly.
➤ Misquoting a verse to someone may affect your credibility if they discover your mistake.

APPLY THE VERSES TO LIFE
➤ Ask God to show how each verse can affect your life and others', whose paths you cross each day, for His glory.
➤ When the verse becomes a part of us, not simply words, we can remember it!

SYSTEMATIC REVIEW
➤ Cement each verse in memory.
➤ Picking one day of the week for reviewing memory verses is helpful. Usually, reviewing a verse for 30 days deepens memory. Get family, friends,

fellow students, neighbors, and co-workers (whether Christian or not) to listen to you recite your verses. If sharing with co-workers, do it only during breaks at work or after work. God's Word will have an impact on others whether we see it or not (see Isaiah 55:11).

➤ You may introduce a friend to Christ without ever directly evangelizing **by relying on** God's Word.

HELPING HANDS

➤ Have you ever been rescued or saved from a dangerous situation?

➤ How did you feel, as you looked up the verses about God the Father loving you?

FAITH STORY
Explain and be prepared to share where you are on your spiritual journey during group time. You'll be in groups of two or three, taking turns sharing your faith story. After sharing with one another, the group will discuss this question: "What is one thing you enjoyed about hearing someone else's faith story?"

If you completed writing your faith story and made a copy for the leader, you can give that to them now.

GROWING TOGETHER

1. What do you believe the following verses say about being a Christian:
   - Isaiah 53:6
   - Romans 5:12
   - Romans 6:23
   - Romans 3:10
   - Acts 4:12
   - Romans 10:9–10
   - Romans 3:23
   - Romans 5:8
   - Ephesians 2:8–9

2. What is the difference between being *religious* and a *follower of Christ*? Possible indicators a person is a Christ-follower:

3. How would you respond if a non-Christian asked you how can you tell if someone is a Christian? Base your answer on the following verses.
   - Romans 8:14–16
   - Galatians 5:22–23

- Romans 10:9–13
- 2 Corinthians 5:17
- Galatians 2:20
- 1 John 2:3–6
- 1 John 3:23–24
- 1 John 4:13–16

4. From viewing the verses in the previous questions (4 and 6), what did you find to be the most comforting, convicting, or challenging? Why?

5. Is it possible or reasonable to expect that a Christian will exhibit these characteristics at all times? Explain (if you can, support your position from Scripture).

CULTIVATING OUR SPIRIT

A cultivated, confident Christ-follower lasts. Please read the following verses:
- Matthew 28:20b
- John 10:27–29
- 2 Corinthians 5:5
- Ephesians 1:13–14

➤ From these verses, what hope can we have in a relationship with Christ?

➤ Did you learn anything new about God?

➤ Would you follow this God? Why or why not?

➤ What makes someone a *Christ follower* or *Christian*?

➤ What are some common misconceptions that people have about what makes someone a Christian?

BEARING FRUIT

Share by reciting these memory verses with one or two others in your group: John 5:24; Romans 6:23; 10:9–10.

And before closing in prayer, share prayer requests, and report answered prayers. Your group leader or facilitator will close in prayer until our *Challenge* session *on* prayer.

DEEPER ROOTS, MORE FRUIT

Be sure to record everything you want to remember in a journal or notebook, in the margins of these pages, or on a computer. You can go back a day from now, or a week, or a year, and see the growth God is giving you in His Word and in following His Spirit.

Cultivating Our Spiritual Passion

OUR OBJECTIVE:
Understanding and beginning to practice the spiritual discipline of spending time alone with God in order to develop a closer relationship with Him.

OUR MEMORY VERSES: 1 Peter 2:2; Psalm 42:1

DAY 1

Have you ever noticed a newborn baby with its mother? What does that baby seem to want to have more than anything else?

➤ According to 1 Peter 2:2, what should our attitude be concerning the Bible?

➤ What example does Psalm 42:1 give us regarding a *passion* for God?

Today's opportunity is to learn or, in some cases, review the benefits of spending time alone with Jesus Christ. And to help practically integrate this time alone with God into our daily schedule. There are principles for learning about God and ourselves. As you view this session, see whether you can practice any of these principles before group time.

➤ "Is it ever difficult for you to add things to your life/schedule?

35

➤ If "Yes," why. If "No," why?

➤ What is the determining factor for whether you add or refuse adding another thing to your life and schedule?"

➤ *Quiet Time* or devotional times are set times for spending time alone with God. They're uninterrupted time to be with God, in order to hear God speak through the Bible, to talk to Him in prayer, and to be prepared by the Holy Spirit for the day.

When do we spend time alone with God? Read the following verses. Write what they communicate to you.

- Psalm 5:3
- Psalm 55:16–17
- Psalm 59:16
- Psalm 88:13
- Psalm 119:147–148
- Mark 1:35

These verses are biblical examples, not commands. You may be a morning person or a night owl. The idea is to start the day with God's blessings and direction.

Psychologists say that our pace for the day is set in the first few minutes of the morning. It's harder to stay consistent at night because we are often tired and our other interests compete with time invested alone with God. For those of us who fight the "battle of the sheets" each morning, here are some helpful suggestions:

1. Decide on a definite time and place to daily meet with God.
2. *Guard the hours for sleep:* It is difficult for most to stay up until 12 a.m. each night and expect to be fresh early the next morning, to hear God speaking to our heart from His Word—the Bible. Medical doctors strongly recommend getting eight hours of sleep—no more, no less. This may not be reality for some: consider adding an extra hour of sleep if you are sleeping less than eight each night.
3. Make sure the alarm on the phone or room clock works.
4. Get up at the alarm, get dressed, and go meet with Jesus.
5. In order to be awake and fresh, exercising or taking a shower before spending time alone with God is helpful.

If you're a night owl, don't force yourself to have morning devotions. Our goal is to have a *quality*, daily quiet time, not to lock ourselves into a box.

The key is giving God our best time for meeting with Him, not leftover time.

DAY 2

Our assignment for today is to determine where to meet with God consistently for some alone time with Him. After reading the verses, record insights you receive.

- Matthew 6:6
- Luke 4:42
- Matthew 14:23
- Mark 1:35

SUGGESTED "DO'S AND DON'TS":

Having quiet time in bed may become *too* quiet! *Do your* quiet time where you can be alone and uninterrupted. Practicing meeting in the same place, at the same time each day can help develop this spiritual discipline.

How long? Any time is better than no time. Consider starting with 15 minutes daily. It's not how much time one spends, but *quality of time with God* and the attitude of heart. We should come to God in *honesty* and *humility*.

DAY 3

Consider dividing your quiet time into 3 segments of 5 minutes; focusing on Bible reading, prayer, and practical application.

➤ Begin with a short prayer, asking God for direction and a teachable spirit. For your first five minutes with God, read the Bible.
➤ During the second five minutes, pray.
➤ And for the final five minutes, take time to meditate—think on and sense—and consider how to make practical personal application of what you read in God's Word.

THE BIBLE

Please read the following verses. In your own words, what do these verses say to you about God's Word and about incorporating daily Bible reading into your quiet time?

- Psalm 119:103–105
- 2 Timothy 3:16–17
- Hebrews 4:12

USING THE BIBLE AS PART OF YOUR QUIET TIME

➤ Consider reading the Bible systematically from Genesis to Revelation. Set a reading goal. A good goal is to read through the Bible once a year; biblegateway.com, or the YouVersion Bible app offer a free reading plan. This will help with seeing the "big picture" of what God has done, is doing, and will do. By averaging about three chapters a day, you'll read the entire Bible in a year! But reading a few verses a day is great too! Decide what works best for you and then do it.

➤ Record scriptural insights and ways that you can apply the Bible to your life. Try to make your application personal, practical, measurable, and attainable. Write them in a journal or in notes on your mobile device.

HERE IS A SAMPLE OF A DAILY QUIET TIME WITH JESUS.

➤ I usually use a school notebook. My wife might buy me a smaller, nicer notebook.

➤ As a morning person, I get up in time to have my devotional time before beginning my commitments for the day.

➤ In my notebook, I record the day's date, whether I'm home or not due to my travel schedule. If on the road, I write the purpose of my trip. Sometimes, I have my quiet time in an airport while waiting on my morning flight (usually before 6 am) and sometimes on the plane.

➤ Then I write, "Praise List." It's really a Praise and Thanksgiving list based on Psalm 68:19, "The Lord daily bears our burdens." I try to recall at least seven things from the previous day to praise God for. Biblical faith isn't blind. I want to *see* how God is working in my life daily. So I mentally rewind the previous day and record events where I felt God acted on my behalf. For example, when I was in college, I would thank God for the games we won. Today, I don't have to score or win. I thank God for playing basketball and not getting hurt! I thank Christ for big or little things. It's all about thanking God for what He does.

➤ I'm reading through the Bible, but I only read a part of the chapter. Typically, I'm reading 1 to 15 verses.

➤ Next, I write *truths* from the verse or verses that I read.

➤ Then, I write *PA* for *practical applications*. I record one truth from what I read that I will try to practice during the day.

➤ Finally, I pray for: my wife, my children, a particular problem I may face, for wisdom, my ministry, and whomever the Holy Spirit might bring to my mind.

<u>Example:</u>

Month/Day/Year	Where: Home or Trip	Purpose of Trip
_____	_____	_____
_____	_____	_____

PRAISE AND THANKSGIVING LIST (EXAMPLES)
➤ Talked with editor about concept, deadline, and meeting concerning publishing disciple-maker workbook
➤ Getting some writing on this project done—numerous distractions
➤ Went with Christina to the park; she wanted me to watch her shoot and see the things she is learning at basketball camp (didn't have time to go, but I couldn't afford not to spend this time with her); she needs to know she comes before my work.
➤ Brenda going to kick-boxing
➤ Time with Michelle and Andrea (other 2 daughters)
➤ Brenda and I making decision with windows man—may be answer to prayer

PSALM 28
➤ Verses 8 and 9: Truths/Insights—the Lord is my strength and He carries me.
➤ Practical application: I need to seek and trust the Lord by asking Him first what to do in my life, as opposed to me trying to do everything first and then seeking His blessings.
➤ Application is the way we can make scriptural truths or insights become a practical part of our lives.
➤ This takes me about 10 to 20 minutes each day. It's seldom I miss spending this time with God, but if I do, I remind myself of God's grace rather than beating up or condemning myself. God is with me!

DAY 4

In the *Challenge* session on prayer, we will dig deeper into this; here, the focus is on prayer as a component of our quiet time.

PRAYER AND PRAISE

We need to spend some time praising God every day. Read the following verses. Write in your own words what they say to you.

- Psalm 34:1
- Matthew 11:25
- Isaiah 61:10
- Luke 1:46–48

If you would like to read more verses on praise, scan the Book of Psalms. Praise is us telling God that we think He is great! It's an expression of our love for Him.

WAYS TO PRAISE GOD:

Praise God for His attributes:

Goodness	Knowledge	Wisdom	Mercy	Power
Holiness	Glory	Grace	Love	Patience

Try reading some of the praise psalms back to God. Psalm 147 is a good example of a praise psalm.

Or you can consider singing praise songs to the Lord. Even if you do not sing "well," the Bible says, "Sing to the Lord" (Psalm 98:1) and "Shout for joy to the Lord" (Psalm 100:1). God is more interested in our heart than the quality of our voice.

DAY 5

Today is an opportunity for us to gain an understanding of the aspects of prayer.

CONFESSION

➤ Read 1 John 1:9.

What does this verse say God will do if we confess our sins?

The word *confession* literally means we are *agreeing with* God that our action (sin) was wrong. We should confess our sins as soon as we are aware we committed sin. As we spend time with God, sometimes He will point out areas of sin that we had not noticed. Sometimes, other Christians will point out sin to us. Be sure to thank the Lord for this and, if a person points a sin out to you, thank that person in a spirit of humility before God.

Repentance is not feeling sorry about our sin (wrongdoing), but to literally *turn our back on the sin* (stop committing the sin). It's changing directions and going God's way. The process of cleansing from sin looks like this:

1. God through the Holy Spirit convicts us.
2. We agree with God that we have done wrong (confess).
3. We choose to do things God's way from now on (repentance).
4. We accept His forgiveness, which Jesus provided for us on the Cross.
5. We thank God for cleansing us.
6. We demonstrate changed action.

THANKSGIVING

Please read the following verses. Record what these verses say to you.

- Romans 8:28
- James 1:2–4
- Philippians 4:4
- Psalm 57
- 1 Thessalonians 5:18

➤ What should the attitude of a follower of Christ be, regardless of circumstances? Why should we exhibit such an attitude?

➤ Notice anything different about David's situation in Psalm 57?

As Christ followers, we should give thanks in all situations. We should spend time thanking God for all He has given us, even for the difficult times in life. Rather than spend most of our time *asking*, we can spend time *thanking* God. We can develop a habit for life of thanking God for people, spiritual blessings, physical abilities, good health, material possessions, and even character–building problems.

INTERCESSION

Intercession is praying for other people's needs. It's one of the highest privileges and responsibilities to which God has called Christians. Even in the Old Testament, it is written, "Far be me it from me that I should sin against the Lord by failing to pray for you" (1 Samuel 12:23). Understand the context here. The Israelites had done something neither God nor Samuel wanted them to do. Yet, Samuel was committed to pray on their behalf anyway.

PRAYER REQUESTS

God, our Father, delights in giving things to His children. A request is asking God for things we need (Matthew 9:11). Our needs may be spiritual, such as wisdom, love, or patience; mental, such as helping us to think more clearly or make a good decision; or physical, such as money, clothes, or rest. God doesn't want us to be afraid to ask Him for anything. No request is too big or small. Philippians 4:6 tells us, "Do not be anxious about anything, but in everything, by prayer and petition, with thanksgiving, present your requests to God."

BEARING FRUIT

Using the acrostic **S-P-A-C-E** can help us discover scriptural insights when we are doing Bible reading.

➢ Is there a **S**in I need to confess?
➢ Is there a **P**romise I need to claim?
➢ Is there an **A**ttitude I need to change?_
➢ Is there a **C**ommand I need to obey?
➢ Is there an **E**xample I need to imitate or eliminate?

You can add to this acrostic, for example, **P** can also represent *prayer*. **E** can also represent an example of something *new* I learned today?

Spending 15 minutes a day with the Lord equals 91 and a half hours a year with God and 76 days alone with God in 20 years. Our prayer can be to grow closer to the Lord as we practice spending quiet time with Him.

Using your notebook or journal, begin to record: "My prayer requests" and "What I need to remember."

DEEPER ROOTS, MORE FRUIT

Between now and the upcoming session, schedule a time to meet with a mature Christian, whom you feel models a lifestyle of serving Jesus as Lord. Interview this person. Before going on your interview, prepare a list of questions to ask, such as:

➢ What would you say is the key for you in following Jesus?

➤ What spiritual disciplines (quiet time, prayer and Bible study) do you regularly practice? How do you go about these practices?

➤ How much time do you think you spend in the Word daily? Why do you think spending time in the Bible should be important to you?

➤ How do you hear from God? Do you have times in your life that you know without a shadow of a doubt that God is speaking to you? How do you know?

➤ Who has been the most influential person in your spiritual development? What is the best thing that person has done for you?

➤ What has helped you the most to mature as a Christian?

➤ Are you growing spiritually? How can you tell? Do you have anyone to whom you are accountable for your spiritual growth? How do they keep you accountable?

➤ When you blow it, how do you get back on track with God?

These are some examples of the kinds of questions you might want to ask. Feel free to use these questions, but also add more of your own.

HELPING HANDS

If you've not already done so, you'll want to memorize our verses for this session. Please see the tips for memorizing verses on pages 31-33.

Reflect (if you can) on the topic of a friendship by discussing the following questions.

➤ Think about *why* someone is your current best friend or about someone who was your best friend when you were growing up. What made them your *best* friend?

➤ What characteristics or traits do you value the most in a close friend?

➤ Which should be part of a person's relationship with Jesus Christ?

Jesus tells us that the greatest commandment is "Love the Lord your God with all your heart and with all your soul and with all your mind" (Matthew 22:37). If we are going to grow in a healthy love relationship with anyone, it requires us to spend time getting to know that person. It's hard to like or love somebody you don't know! As we work through this session, think about this question: *Am I willing to adjust my schedule in order to spend personal time with God?*

GROWING TOGETHER

To grow in our relationship with God, we need to spend time with Him regularly. Quiet time is set, uninterrupted time in our schedule to be with God in order to hear God speak through the Bible, to talk to God in prayer, and for the Holy Spirit to prepare us for the day ahead.

1. *Read* 1 Corinthians 1:9. What does this verse say to you? How would you define the word *fellowship*?
2. *What* do you generally consider to be your best time of the day? Why?
3. *When* is a good time to meet with God? Read the following verses: Psalms 5:3; 55:16–17; 119:147–148; Mark 1:35. According to these verses, what do you think is the key to making this so? How much of a challenge is it for you to try to spend time alone with God on a regular basis?
4. *Where?* Read the following verses: Matthew 6:6; Mark 6:46; Luke 4:42a. What is so crucial about where a person spends personal time with God? When it comes to spending time alone with God, where do you tend to feel closest to God? Why?
5. *When* you spend quiet time with God, what things do you generally do as part of this time? Or if you have never spent quiet time alone with God, but want to, what would you want to do during this time alone with God?
6. *Why* should regularly spending time in God's Word be a part of our lives? Read Matthew 4:4. How have you have benefitted from reading the Bible?
7. *When* it comes to prayer, what is a model or example you have found helpful? Why?
8. *What* are some practical methods we can apply to our lives related to what we hear from God when we pray and read our Bible?

CULTIVATING OUR SPIRIT

Reconsider these Scriptures: Mark 1:35; Philippians 3:10.

Before praying within your group, you'll share prayer requests. Be sure to include any updates to requests you shared in the previous sessions.

BEARING FRUIT

Have a quiet time several times this week (every day, if you can). Set a goal. If you miss a day or even two, it's not the end of the world. Give yourself some grace. Don't let your meeting with God become a burden or some religious duty. Work on establishing consistency. *Be realistic.* Set aside a specific amount of time. To start, you may want to for plan fifteen minutes. (Refer to the suggested 15 minutes quiet time agenda and ideas for incorporating the Bible, prayer, and practical application into your quiet time.)

If it would help you to achieve the goal you set, ask a friend to help hold you accountable. Give this person your schedule, and ask them to ask about your progress throughout the week. You can share with them what you learned about God, Jesus Christ, or yourself.

Understanding the Holy Spirit

OUR OBJECTIVE:
Learning who the Person of the Holy Spirit is, how He functions in the life of a follower of Christ, and how He functions with God the Father and Jesus Christ, the Son.

OUR MEMORY VERSES: Galatians 2:20; Ephesians 5:17–18

DAY 1

Today is about discovering who the Holy Spirit really is. Please look up the following verses. For each, write what it says to you about who the Holy Spirit is.

- Matthew 28:19
- John 14:16–17
- John 15:26
- John 16:13–15

DAY 2

Have you heard the term *Trinity* in relation to God? If this term has been confusing in the past, it will become a little clearer today. *Trinity* is used to explain the relationship between the Holy Spirit, God the Father, and Jesus the Son. Another name for the Trinity is the *Godhead*.

Who is present in the following passages?

- Matthew 3:16–17
- Mark 1:9–11
- Luke 3:21–22
- 1 Corinthians 6:11
- 2 Corinthians 13:14

For the following verses, how do we see the Holy Spirit at work with Jesus during His time on earth?

- Luke 4:1
- Luke 4:14–19
- John 1:32–34
- Romans 8:11

DAY 3

Let's see and record from these verses how the Holy Spirit functions, and His purpose.

- John 14:25–27
- John 16:7–8
- John 16:13–14
- Acts 1:8
- Romans 8:1–2
- Romans 8:9
- Romans 8:11
- Romans 8:15–17
- Romans 8:26–27
- Ephesians 1:13–14

Let's take a closer look at Luke 1:9–11; who is present? There seems to be a hierarchical ranking and order within the Trinity. Do these verses help you or raise questions?

- John 14:6
- John 14:9–11
- John 14:28–31
- John 16:13–15
- John 17:1, 4–5, 20–23

DAY 4

Let's evaluate our spiritual health—allowing the Holy Spirit to guide us. (We will also often refer to the Holy Spirit as simply the Spirit.)

➤ Rejecting the Spirit's influence: Read Romans 8:5–17 and Galatians 5:15–26. List what actions, acts, and attitudes characterize our sinful nature (a nature disobedient to God—the Holy Spirit).

➤ Review your list. Take a few minutes to prayerfully reflect on these questions: *Am I seeing these things in my life? If "Yes," how?*

➤ Allowing the Spirit's influence: Revisit Romans 8:5–17 and Galatians 5:15–26. Record what actions and attitudes characterize living by (following) the Spirit:

➤ Reviewing your list, take a few minutes to prayerfully reflect on these questions:

➤ *Am I seeing these things in my life? If "Yes," how?*

DAY 5

Today we will understand more about how to follow (yield and submit to) the Spirit, because He won't force us to obey. And we'll see how to avoid, as much as possible, causing the Spirit to grieve. When we try living our life on our own, we sin and cause the Holy Spirit to grieve. Please read Ephesians 4:31–5:11, and record what actions *grieve* the Holy Spirit.

So, what can a Christian do, who sins and grieves the Spirit? Do we have a quiet time seven days in a row? Do we become more active in church? Do we memorize more Bible verses? Even though these are good things, doing them to try to excuse or make up for our sin is wrong. We can do nothing apart from God to gain forgiveness for our sin. We simply have to yield ourselves to God, the Holy Spirit.

The key to living by the Spirit is being *filled* (empowered) *by* the Holy Spirit. Ephesians 5:18 instructs us to be "filled with the Spirit." As you complete your preparation for the upcoming group session, ask God to walk with you and empower you through His Holy Spirit.

1. *Understand* that the Holy Spirit lives inside of each and every person who is a Christian. Galatians 4:6 tells us, "Because you are sons [and daughters], God sent the Spirit of His Son into our hearts, the Spirit who calls out, 'Abba, Father.'" Also read Romans 8:9.

2. *Consider* that God desires for you to submit completely to the Holy Spirit. This is how you experience the abundant life mentioned in John 10:10.

3. *Repent* of any sin in your life. To *repent* literally is to turn your back on the sin and stop doing the sin. It does not mean to feel sorry for your disobedience, yet continue repeating it. Repentance should follow confession. Confession is saying in agreement with God that our sin is wrong. See 1 John 1:9

4. *Reject* sinful desires which keep you from experiencing God's best. Pray for Galatians 2:20 and Philippians 4:13 to be a consistent reality in your life.

5. *Yield* to the Holy Spirit. We receive the Holy Spirit by faith at salvation, to continue to live by faith in relationship to the Holy Spirit. "So I say, live by the Spirit, and you will not gratify the desires of the sinful nature…Since we live by the Spirit, let us keep in step with the Spirit" (Galatians 5:16, 25).

6. *Enjoy* the blessings of the Holy Spirit. Read the following passages, recording the blessings that come from the Holy Spirit: John 15:5–11; Galatians 5:22–25.

DEEPER ROOTS, MORE FRUIT

Write a prayer, asking God to empower you to yield your life totally to the leading of the Holy Spirit.

HELPING HANDS

We'll join in opening this time in a brief prayer for your group and your time together, and then discuss how the week went and engage in a visual activity. We will work with partners to complete a task involving drawing.

Everyone will pair up with a partner, sitting back-to-back so that one person in each pair is facing the group leader and the other is not. Each person facing away from the leader will be a designated "artist"; the artists will need paper and pen. Each person facing the leader will be a "describer."

Once everyone is situated, the leader will show the describers a picture, and in turn the describers will tell the artists what to draw. You'll have two minutes to work with your partner to complete this task. After time is called, artists can turn around and see what they were supposed to be drawing. Compare drawings, then discuss these questions:

➤ What made this activity difficult? Easy?

➤ How did you feel about your partner as you worked together?

➤ Briefly describe a time someone had to guide you so you could accomplish a task or reach a goal. How did that feel?

➤ Report on your experience with last session's Deeper Roots, More Fruit.

GROWING TOGETHER

➤ How would you explain to a friend who the Holy Spirit is? Revisit John 14:28, 31; John 14:13, 24; John 17:1, 3.

➤ How would you characterize the relationship between God, Jesus, and the Holy Spirit?

➤ What does each verse or verses say about the role of the Holy Spirit in your life?
  - Matthew 28:19
  - John 14:16
  - John 15:26
  - John 14:16–17
  - John 16:13–15
  - Acts 1:8
  - Romans 8:1–2
  - Romans 8:9
  - Romans 8:15–17
  - Romans 8:26–27
  - Ephesians 1:13–14
  - 1 John 4:13–18

➤ Based on these passages, describe the role of the Holy Spirit and what it includes?

➤ Of all the roles the Holy Spirit wants to play in your life, which one do you need to appreciate the most right now? Why?

➤ How should we live? In group time, we'll talk about one of these passages: Romans 8:5–17; Galatians 5:15–26.

During group time, we'll compare and contrast life by the Spirit and life by the sinful nature and see the consequences of living to the sinful nature and living to the Spirit.

➤ Let's look at trusting the Holy Spirit. Read John 15:1–11. What is required to live a life yielded to the Holy Spirit? Practically, how can we do this?

➤ Please read Galatians 5:22–25 again. What specific blessings come from living by the Spirit? What is the key to experiencing the fruit of the Spirit in your life?

➤ Spend a quiet moment thinking about your day. Have you displayed the fruit of the Spirit in your actions and attitudes? Is there any "pruning" God needs to do so you can consistently allow the Holy Spirit to work in your life? Prayerfully, reflect in silence about what those things might be.

CULTIVATING OUR SPIRIT

Share these verses from memory with others in your group: Galatians 2:20 and Ephesians 5:17–18.

Talking to God: Share prayer requests. Be sure to include any updates to requests that you shared in previous sessions. You can keep a prayer notebook to record how God is answering the prayers of your group.

BEARING FRUIT

In Ephesians 5:18, Paul encourages us to be "filled with the Spirit." The key to letting the Holy Spirit influence our actions and attitude is to be filled (empowered) by the Holy Spirit. We discovered that the Holy Spirit wants to work in and through us in many ways.

This coming week, look for the Holy Spirit to be at work daily in your world. See if you have a memorable experience in which you feel the Holy Spirit is involved.

MONDAY: READ JOHN 14:16–17
Jesus says the Holy Spirit will be our *Paraclete*, which is translated as "counselor." This Greek term—*paraclete*—means a whole lot more, including helper, comforter, teacher, and someone to walk with you. In what ways did the Holy Spirit comfort you today?

TUESDAY: READ JOHN 16:12–15
The Holy Spirit wants to lead us to understanding the truth about Jesus and God. In what ways did your knowledge of God and faith deepen today?

WEDNESDAY: READ ACTS 1:4–9
The Holy Spirit brought power into the lives of Jesus' disciples. The Holy Spirit helps believers lead powerful, God-honoring lives. In what ways did you see the Holy Spirit bring power into your life today?

THURSDAY: READ ROMANS 8:1–2
Many people lead lives of guilt and shame. But because of Jesus' sacrifice, we're free from relying on our own goodness to please God. The Holy Spirit helps us experience the freedom of being new in Christ. In what ways did you experience the reality of God's grace today?

FRIDAY: READ ROMANS 8:8–9; 15–17
The Holy Spirit reminds us that we belong to Jesus. In what way, today, did you experience the reality of being a child of God through Jesus Christ?

SATURDAY: READ EPHESIANS 1:13–14.
The Holy Spirit is in one aspect, a "down payment" preparing us for the day when we'll always be with God. In what ways, today, were you reminded of what's it's like to be with God?

SUNDAY: READ 1 JOHN 4:13–18.
God is love, and the Holy Spirit wants you to know God even more intimately. How did you feel God's love today? You may have to think hard if you had a bad day today. Not every day is a good day, but there is good in every day.

Praying—Talking With God

OUR OBJECTIVE:
Helping us as Christ followers to become better acquainted with Him through the *two-way*, supernatural, dynamic fellowship of communicating with God. Prayer is a way of life, not a religious function.

OUR MEMORY VERSES: John 15:7; Philippians 4:6–7

DAY 1

Today's goal is simply to gain a better understanding of prayer and its priority for Jesus Christ's followers. In Paul's letter of instruction about ministry, he told young Timothy, "I urge, then, *first* of all, to pray for all people. Ask God to help them; intercede on their behalf, and give thanks for them" (1 Timothy 2:1, emphasis author's).

> "Prayer does not fit us for the greater works, prayer *is* the greater work. We, as ordinary human beings, have the ability to change ourselves, our families, our churches, our friends, and our communities from our 'prayer closets' because when we enter into true prayer, we touch the heart of God with whom all things are possible. The greatest thing we as Christians can learn to do is *pray*. Did I say learn? Yes. The only way that we learn to pray is by praying. We can do conferences on prayer, read books about prayer, and hear sermons on prayer, but until we learn to daily come before God ourselves, we will *never* learn the art of prayer."
> —OSWALD CHAMBERS, author, *My Utmost for His Highest*

TALKING TO GOD
Prayer is usually defined as a two-way communication with God: talking *and* listening.

➤ Read Matthew 6:13–19.
  Jesus Christ is teaching His disciples how to pray. This prayer has been memorized by many and is often quoted during worship services; but

we see the primary purpose is to teach us how to pray *specifically*. Write down the specific elements of prayer.

➤ What do these verses say to us about prayer: Psalm 55:22; Philippians 4:6–7; 1 Peter 5:7?

LISTENING TO GOD

Look up the following verses. For each, write in your own words what it communicates to you.

- Psalm 5:3
- Isaiah 30:21
- Jeremiah 33:3
- John 10:3–5, 27

DAY 2

Some say praying is difficult. Yesterday's last three verses motivate most Christ followers to pray. Let's discover why we should pray, and what are possible barriers to prayer.

> "A man may pray night and day and deceive himself, but no man can be assured of his sincerity who does not pray. *Prayer is faith passing into action.* A union of the will and intellect realizing in an intelligent act. It is the whole man that prays. Less than this is wishing or lip work, a sham. . . ."
>
> —RICHARD CECIL

➤ List reasons why you might have a difficult time praying.

Look up the following verses. For each, write what each passage says to you.

- Psalm 145:18
- Matthew 26:41
- 1 Thessalonians 5:17
- Matthew 7:7–8
- Mark 1:35
- Hebrews 4:16
- Matthew 18:18–20
- Luke 21:36
- James 5:16

> We must remember that the goal of prayer is the ear of God. Unless that is gained the prayer has utterly failed. The utterings of it may have kindled devotional feelings in our minds, the bearing of it may have comforted and strengthened the hearts of those with

whom we have prayed, but if the prayer has not gained the heart of God, it has failed in its essential purpose.

— CHARLES H. SPURGEON, preacher and author

How do we get the ear of God? By being honest with ourselves as we talk with God. We don't have to try to sound like a preacher, deacon, or spiritual person to gain access to God. If we are praying in public, we don't have to try to impress the audience. In fact, pretend it is only God and you.

DAY 3

God answers our prayers; yes, no, and wait. In Mark 14:35–36, Jesus is asking God the Father to change His mind about Jesus' dying on the cross. God says no to His Son's request! God says no to Paul in 2 Corinthians 12:7–10. In Luke 18:1–8, His answer is wait, with an eventual yes, but no timetable is given. James 4:3 shows us that we need the right motives when we pray. First John 5:14–15 is a yes, if we pray according to His Will, but again, no timetable. For every verse, write what you believe each says regarding the ways God answers prayer, and why.

- Mark 14:35–36
- Luke 18:1–8
- 2 Corinthians 12:7–10
- James 5:16–18
- James 4:3
- 1 John 5:14–15

QUESTIONS ABOUT PRAYER

Read each Scripture passage below. What can or should we ask for in prayer, in what context, and what results should we expect?

Scripture: 2 Chronicles 7:14:

Request: _____

Context: _____

Expected result: _____

To what nation does this verse apply? _____

Does this biblical principle apply to us today? _____

Scripture: John 14:12–14

Request: _____

Context: _____

Expected result: _____

SCRIPTURE: JOHN 15:7–8
Request: _____
Context: _____
Expected result: _____

SCRIPTURE: JOHN 16:24
Request: _____
Context: _____
Expected result: _____

SCRIPTURE: 1 JOHN 5:14–15
Request: _____
Context: _____
Expected result: _____

DAY 4

Today, we'll see more reasons He sometimes says no to some of our prayers. And what we may need to do in order for God to say "Yes" to our prayers.

Please find the Scripture passages listed. For each verse and passage listed, identify why God may say no to our prayers and what personal change(s) you may need to make. You may not need to make a personal change for every verse/passage, if it doesn't apply to you.

SCRIPTURE: JOB 35:12–13
Reason: _____
Personal change needed:_____

SCRIPTURE: PSALM 66:18
Reason: _____
Personal change needed:_____

SCRIPTURE: PSALM 139:23–24
Reason: _____
Personal change needed:_____

SCRIPTURE: MATTHEW **6:33**
Reason: _____
Personal change needed: _____

SCRIPTURE: MARK **11:25–26**
Reason: _____
Personal change needed: _____

SCRIPTURE: EPHESIANS **6:12**
Reason: _____
Personal change needed: _____

SCRIPTURE: JAMES **1:6–8**
Reason: _____
Personal change needed: _____

SCRIPTURE: JAMES **4:3**
Reason: _____
Personal change needed: _____

DAY 5

There are certain Scripture passages that contain God's promises to us, but we must ask or pray for them. Please read the scriptures listed. For each, identify God's promise and any change(s) you may need to make in your life.

Scripture	God's Promise	Change I Need to Make
(Example) Isaiah 26:3	*perfect peace*	*I need to focus on God more than me*
● Psalm 37:4		
● Jeremiah 29:11–12		
● Isaiah 40:31		
● Matthew 6:33		
● 1 Corinthians 10:13		
● 2 Corinthians 2:14		
● Philippians 4:6–7		
● Ephesians 1:3		
● 2 Thessalonians 3:3		

Scripture	God's Promise	Change I Need to Make
(Example) Isaiah 26:3	*perfect peace*	*I need to focus on God more than me*

- James 4:7–8a
- 1 John 4:4
- 1 John 4:18
- 1 John 5:4–5
- 1 John 5:18 (read NABS or NLT translation)

"Prayer [is] nothing else but a sense of the presence of God."
—BROTHER LAWRENCE, author, *Practicing the Presence of God*

DEEPER ROOTS, MORE FRUIT

Dedicate time to prayer, putting into practice the lessons learned from the day's prayer teachings and activities this week.

HELPING HANDS

For openers, your group will stand in a circle. A leader will begin the activity. A single message will be whispered (by the leader first to the person to his or her right), and likewise repeated, as a whisper, to the next person in the circle, until the message makes it all the way around the circle and back to the leader. You'll then discuss the following questions:

➢ How did the original message compare to the final one?
➢ What would have made this game easier?
➢ What are some keys to good communication?
➢ What would you say are some keys to effective communication with God?

Report on your experience with Deeper Roots, More Fruit.

GROWING TOGETHER

➢ Who is someone you admire as a person of prayer? What is it about this person that makes him or her a person of prayer in your eyes?
➢ How would you define *prayer*? Why?
➢ Please read John 14:13–14. What is one goal of prayer?

➤ When do you find yourself praying most often?

➤ Under what circumstances do you have a hard time praying?

➤ List some reasons as to why praying could be difficult?

Your group will divide the following Scriptures among three or four groups, read your verses, and discuss reasons for prayer, then report insights.

● Psalm 145:18	● Luke 21:36
● Jeremiah 33:3	● Philippians 4:6–7
● Matthew 7:7–8	● 1 Thessalonians 5:17
● Matthew 18:18–20	● Hebrews 4:16
● Matthew 26:41	● James 1:5–8
● Luke 11:2–4	● James 5:16

➤ How many different ways would you say God answers prayer? (If you can, support your statement with an example—a Bible verse or passage, or an example from your own experience.)

CULTIVATING OUR SPIRIT

➤ Read John 15:7; 1 John 5:14–15.

➤ According to these verses, what are some key conditions to effective prayer? Practically, how can we meet these conditions in our prayers?

➤ Have you ever experienced the power of prayer in your life? Would you like to share it?

➤ Read the following promises from God:

● Psalm 55:22	● James 4:7–8a
● Proverbs 3:5–6	● 1 John 1:9
● Isaiah 40:31	● 1 John 4:4
● 1 Corinthians 10:130	● 1 John 4:18
● Philippians 4:13	● 1 John 5:4–5
● Luke 11:2–4	● James 5:16

➤ Which Scripture promise (from the preceding verses or from the verses we reviewed for question 7), do you most need to claim in your life? Spend a minute in silent prayer.

BEARING FRUIT

John 15:7; Philippians 4:6–7 are our memory verses to share during this time.

Share prayer requests and pray together. Your group leader will help your group consider *conversational* praying.

The following prayer outline, divided by days of the week, is designed to help you pray daily in the coming week:

➤ Every day—Pray for spouse, if married, and any immediate family.
➤ Sunday—Pray for church staff and government leaders.
➤ Monday—Pray for extended family.
➤ Tuesday—Pray for close friends.
➤ Wednesday—Pray for fellow church members.
➤ Thursday—Pray for neighbors and co-workers.
➤ Friday—Pray for acquaintances and friends who may not know Christ.
➤ Saturday—Pray for non-Christians and opportunities to tell them about Jesus.

Finding a mature Christian, who likes to pray, can be a real encouragement. Ask them to share why they like to pray and how prayer has benefited their life. You may also want to team up with another person or two in your group to meet and pray. "For where two or three come together in my name, there am I with them" (Matthew 18:20).

PART 2 GROWING

BOWING TO LORD JESUS

WEARING GOD-GLASSES

FORGIVING AND
HEALTHIER LIVING

GROWING
DEEPER
ROOTS

Bowing to Lord Jesus

OUR OBJECTIVE:
To understand the lordship of Christ and to experience this daily.

OUR MEMORY VERSES: Luke 9:23–25; 6:46

DAY 1

What are considerations for Jesus Christ's lordship? At the core of being a *disciple* is the truth that Jesus Christ is *Lord of Life*. As each of us completes this challenge, we will pray and ask God to help us evaluate where we are spiritually, and *why*. As Christians, the issue isn't whether or not God lives in us through the Person of the Holy Spirit. Rather, the question each of us must ask is: Am I allowing Jesus Christ to *lead me as Lord of my life*?

As we begin, let's ask ourselves: *Are there any areas of my life—priorities, time with God, family, friendships, commitment to church, work, recreation-hobbies, and so on—where Jesus is* not *Lord?*

If you're not a Christ follower, but you do believe you are on a spiritual journey, please evaluate where you are and why.

➤ Why He's Lord. According to the following verses, why should Jesus Christ be considered Lord? Isaiah 45:12, Ephesians 2:10 and Revelation 4:11.

➤ According to the following verses, Isaiah 52:14, 53:2–7, 12d; and Romans 14:8, are there additional reasons for Jesus Christ to be considered Lord?

➤ Why else could Jesus Christ be considered Lord, according to these verses?
- John 1:11–13
- Ephesians 1:5
- Romans 8:15–16
- Galatians 4:5

➤ Has Jesus Christ earned the right to be your Lord? Why or why not?

DEFINING *LORDSHIP*
The word, *lord*, as described in a dictionary can be:
➤ a person who has authority, control, or power over others; a master, chief, or ruler.

➤ a person who exercises authority from property rights; an owner of land, houses, etc.

➤ a person who is a leader, or has great influence in a chosen profession: *the great lords of banking.*

➤ a feudal superior; the proprietor of a manor.

➤ a titled nobleman or peer; a person whose ordinary appellation contains by courtesy the title *Lord* or some higher title.

Find other titles or synonyms for *lord*:

DAY 2

What is required to experience Jesus Christ's lordship? Read Luke 9:23–25 to find out. In an individualistic or *"all-about-me"* culture, what do those verses communicate? Jesus requires three commitments (maybe four) His followers must make to experience His lordship. What are they?

➤ What do you think Jesus means when He says a follower of His must deny *himself* or *herself?*

➤ What does Jesus mean when He says His followers *must take up their cross?*

➤ When we mention "taking up your cross," people think about Christian responsibilities as burden. Taking up our cross also includes experiencing all God has to offer Christ followers: privileges and blessings.

➤ What is involved in *following Jesus?* (Read Mark 1:17; 3:31–34; Luke 14:26; Matthew 8:18–22.)

➤ What does a Jesus-as-Lord disciple look like? Record the principles in the following Scriptures:

- Psalm 82:3–4
- Proverbs 14:31
- Psalm 1:2
- Joshua 1:8
- Mark 1:35
- Matthew 20:25–28
- Galatians 5:22–23
- 1 Peter 3:15
- 1 Peter 3:8–12
- 1 Peter 4:12–19
- 1 John 1:9
- 1 Corinthians 16:1–2

How do we experience Jesus Christ's lordship? A common phrase among the church community regarding Jesus' lordship is that we *make Jesus Lord*. However, *we* don't *make* Jesus Lord; He *is* Lord. We *submit* to the lordship of Jesus Christ. Rather than an emotional response, we submit to Christ's lordship by an act of will. See the following verses and note what each says:

- Matthew 6:33
- Psalm 42:1
- Luke 6:46
- John 14:12, 15
- Matthew 28:19–20

What does John 13:34–35 tell us about Christ's lordship in action? God demonstrates His love through us. Let's say we love our neighbor Tom. We can first tell Tom we love him as a friend or a person. And then we can help landscape his yard this Saturday. Such an act makes our love tangible, manageable, and attainable. Does this make sense to you? Why or why not?

Luke 9:22 tells of Jesus Christ's suffering, rejection, death, and His ultimate resurrection.

Therefore, living out the lordship of Christ may include all aspects of commitment. See also Philippians 3:10. As you study Luke 9:23–25, it becomes apparent that denying yourself, taking up His cross, and following Him is not optional. Christians are to obey these commands.

Getting involved in this challenge results in fulfillment in life: "Whoever would lose his life for My sake will find it" (Luke 9:24). But not meeting His challenge and living for self is how a person loses life, fulfillment, and significance. "Whoever would save his life will lose it" (v. 24). It's the difference between existing and living.

> [After becoming a Christian] "I loved all mankind, slaveholders not excepted, though I abhorred slavery more than ever. I saw the world in a new light . . . I have gathered scattered pages of the Bible from filthy street gutters, and washed and dried them, that in moments of leisure I might get a word or two of wisdom from them."
> —FREDERICK DOUGLASS, abolitionist, author, orator, ex-slave

This great man demonstrated characteristics of a Christ follower who is yielding to the lordship of Jesus Christ. His words revealed both his forgiveness of those who enslaved him and a passion for God's Word.

DAY 3

Demonstrations of Jesus Christ's lordship:

➤ Joseph was sold into slavery by his brothers, the sons of Joseph's father, Jacob and Jacob's wife, Leah. Later, the prison administrator's wife lied about Joseph, resulting in his wrongful imprisonment (see Genesis chapters 37—39). Yet in Genesis 40:1–23, what attribute of our Lord did Joseph demonstrate?

➤ Imagine being an orphan, part of a despised minority, rising to the position of queen, then having your uncle ask you to risk everything, including your life. What attribute of our Lord do we see modeled by Queen Esther? Read Esther 4:1–16.

➤ Read Luke 10:25–37.
What attribute of lordship does the Good Samaritan reveal?

➤ Rahab was an outcast and a prostitute rejected by society. Read Joshua 6:17 and record what attribute of lordship she demonstrated.

➤ Anna was a widow. She was 84 years old and a prophetess. How did she model the same attribute that Rahab had? Read Luke 2:36–38.

➤ Why might Jonah have so strongly resisted going to Nineveh? The people of Nineveh had certainly persecuted and most likely killed some of his relatives. So when he finally went to Nineveh what attribute of lordship did Jonah demonstrate (Jonah 3)?

➤ Read Luke 7:36–38 and John 12:1–3.
What attribute of lordship do Mary, the sister of Lazarus, and the woman in Luke model?

➤ Read John 14: 22–33.
Peter seems to be a lot like us in this. What does the Bible reveal?

➤ Ruth entered a new city as a foreigner and outsider, but her living out this attribute of lordship gave her favor in her new surroundings. Read Ruth 2:11. What is that attribute?

➤ Zacchaeus had become wealthy by defrauding others. After encountering Jesus, Zacchaeus vowed to restore his relationship through what attribute? Read Luke 19:1–10.

➤ Paul, a godly leader, lost respect for and trust in John Mark, a young minister. Read Acts 15:36–40. What happened?

➤ Read 2 Timothy 4:11. What attribute did Paul demonstrate?

➤ Read Matthew 1:18–25.
This young couple is going against their beliefs and cultures, resulting in being shamed. What attribute of lordship is worth this humiliation?

➤ Do you see any of these attributes of lordship in your life? Which ones? And with which ones do you struggle?

Jesus came to give glory to His Father. *"Father . . . glorify your Son, that your Son may glorify you."* John 17:1

Since Jesus is Lord, we are to glorify the Father through Jesus Christ. As a trophy glorifies the person who won, the life of the person of whom Jesus is Lord gives glory and praise to Jesus. This happens when every aspect of our being surrenders to His purposes.

These attributes or characteristics belong to Jesus Christ. Since we belong to Him, we develop the same characteristics. As we continue making ourselves available to Jesus Christ as Lord, these characteristics will reproduce themselves in our lives.

HINDRANCES

The more we understand the lordship of Christ, the more we will understand that we Christians are Christ's servants. Experiencing Christ's lordship is a choice. It is a choice we make everyday, all day long. We don't *make* Christ Lord. He *is* Lord whether we want Him to be or not! The issue of whether we *experience* Christ as Lord in our daily lives depends on our yielding and submitting to His lordship. Jesus Christ will not force His lordship on us. Read Revelation 3:20.

Our decision to yield to Christ's lordship may be met with interference. The following is a list of possible issues, which can hinder us from experiencing Jesus Christ as Lord.

- Worry
- Talk (tongue)—profanity, cruel words, and more
- Thought-life (negativity and complaining)
- Critical spirit (fault-finding)
- Temper
- A poor self-image (not seeing self in the way God does)
- Self-pity (another result of not seeing yourself the way God does)
- Withdrawing—through alcohol, drugs, pornography, and other addictions
- Sex (before or outside of marriage)
- Envy
- Self-effort
- Fear
- Manipulation—putting others before ourselves for the wrong reasons
- Money
- Priorities
- Pride
- Pleasure
- Position

➤ Is anything on this list hindering you from experiencing Christ as Lord in your life? Can you think of any other possible interferences for you?

DAY 4

Lordship without *legalism;* this is where our theology becomes reality. We must now act on what we know. Yet, in our imperfection, *how* do we live out "Christ as Lord"?

➤ Which one of the Bible personalities do you most relate to in the area of lordship? Why?

➤ What do you think they did to demonstrate lordship at that particular time in their lives?

67

➤ What do you think you need to do to experience lordship in the areas of your life where you struggle?

To experience the lordship of Christ, first we need to believe that He knows what is best for our life. Next, it is simply an act of our will. We choose Christ. This choice requires putting Christ Jesus first in our life, even before family and ourselves. Such a choice doesn't require us to forget about our family or ourselves. It is realizing that the God of the universe loves us more than we love ourselves and has the *best* plan for our lives! Knowing Jesus as Lord starts with a personal relationship with Jesus as Savior.

That alone results in the Holy Spirit (often described as the indwelling Holy Spirit) living inside of us. We will never be alone!

Maybe you joined this discipleship *Challenge* because you have been on a spiritual journey. Your journey has led you here. If you have never done this and want to, follow the steps here. Make these steps with your heart and mind. Establishing a personal relationship with Jesus Christ is very easy and simple.

➤ First, each person must believe that God created humanity (Adam and Eve) as the crowning achievement of all of His creation. Until Adam and Eve disobeyed God, they had perfect fellowship with Him. The consequence of their sin was death, but God didn't kill them. God showed them grace and mercy. Instead, he banished them from the Garden of Eden.

➤ God sent His only Son, Jesus Christ, who was fully God—who simultaneously was human—and lived a sinless life, despite being tempted in every way. Then Jesus paid the penalty of our sin by dying on the cross for every person's sin (the born and yet-to-be born), in the place of all humanity, you and me.

➤ Then the Holy Spirit (Romans 8:11) raised Jesus Christ from the dead on the third day to have victory over death.

➤ Now, you and I can have eternal life with Jesus Christ by simply asking Him to forgive us of our sin (we were born in sin because of Adam—father of all mankind) and to come into our life and make it what He wants it to be. It is just that simple.

➤ It is an act of faith. If we are sincere in our response to Him, God in the Person of the Holy Spirit will come to live inside of us.

Read the following verses found in the Book of Romans:

"Therefore, just as sin entered the world through one man, and death through sin, and in this way death came to all men, because all sinned." ROMANS 5:12

"There is none righteous, not even one." ROMANS 3:10

"For all have sinned and fall short of the glory of God." ROMANS 3:23

"But God demonstrates His love for us in this: While we were still sinners, Christ died for us." ROMANS 5:8

"For the wages of sin is death, but the gift of God is eternal life in Christ Jesus our Lord." ROMANS 6:23

"That if you confess with your mouth, 'Jesus is Lord,' and believe in your heart that God raised Him [Jesus Christ] from the dead, you will be saved [rescued/delivered]. For it is with your heart that you believe and are justified, and it is with your mouth that you confess [agree with God] and are saved." ROMANS 10:9-10

If this is the *desire of your heart*, simply ask Jesus Christ to forgive you for your sins and to come into your life as your Savior and Lord right now, and He will. This act isn't based on emotions or feeling, but the truth of God's Word.

A prayer for a personal relationship with Jesus Christ

Lord Jesus, I need You. Thank You for dying on the cross for my sins. I admit that I am a sinner and separated from You. Please forgive me. I receive You as my Savior and Lord. Thank You for forgiving my sins and giving me eternal life. Please take control of my life. Make me the kind of person You want me to be. Amen.

If you just prayed this prayer, "There is joy in the presence of God's angels" (Luke 15:10). Having Christ in our heart is the difference, and a necessary step for experiencing Christ's lordship.

DAY 5

We can proceed with how we can *experience* lordship when we are sure about our personal relationship with Jesus Christ. It's good knowing that the Holy Spirit will guide and give peace to every believer. We read in Galatians 5:22–23, the fruit of having the Holy Spirit, including experiencing God's peace.

After we become a follower of Christ or a Christian, we may disobey God. When a child or teenager disobeys his or her parent, that child or teenager doesn't cease to be a son or daughter of that parent. The love relationship doesn't change, but the fellowship of that relationship can change drastically. And the child will have to ask for forgiveness.

➤ According to 1 John 1:9, what are we to do when we sin, disobeying God?

➤ Please read Psalm 103:12 and write what it says.

➤ Each morning, we can ask the Holy Spirit to guide our plans for the day. According to Proverbs 16:3, what should we do with our plans?

➤ Summarize what Proverbs 16:1, 9; 19:21 tell us about our plans.

➤ According to previous verses and Proverbs 16:4, why can we trust God?

➤ If we are to experience Jesus as our Lord, there are certain actions we can do that will help us. But our actions are not to become a *religion*. Based on Joshua 1:8 and Psalm 1:2, how often should we read our Bibles?

Having daily disciplines, like time with God (Jeremiah 33:3) and praying to God will bless you as well as those who come into contact with you. So will some of the activities, such as studying your Bible, telling someone you know about Jesus Christ who doesn't know Him, memorizing Scripture, and regularly experiencing corporate worship (Hebrews 10:24–25) in a Bible-teaching church. These will be invaluable to you.

As we become closer to Christ by practicing spiritual disciplines, our prayer life will become a stalwart force in our relationship with Him. One way we can grow strong in faith and trust in Christ is to keep a record of our prayers and how they are answered. At some point, you will be able to see how God's answer produced fruit.

PRAYER REQUEST PAGE

NAME	PRAYER REQUEST	DATE	HOW ANSWERED	DATE

DEEPER ROOTS, MORE FRUIT

Consider having a mature Christian(s), to whom you are accountable, and who will ask you personal questions about your life. These are people with whom you can be honest! Mature Christians don't have to be older in years; but strong or growing in their faith.

➤ How does having Jesus Christ as Lord of your life make you more productive for God's glory?

➤ Memorize, if you have not done so already: Luke 9:23–25; 6:46

HELPING HANDS

Share with your group those you consider *ultimate bosses*. Your choices don't have to be limited to the business world. Think of those who appear to have incredible control of their companies, institutions, or situations. Explain your choices.

➤ Are you or would you like to be an ultimate boss? Why or why not?

➤ Report on your experience with last session's Deeper Roots, More Fruit. What does the phrase, "filled with the Holy Spirit," communicate to you?

GROWING TOGETHER

➤ Discuss:
1. Do you think Jesus Christ has a *right* to be our Lord? Why or why not?

2. What comes to your mind when you hear this concept?

3. Do you have a difficult time embracing this term? Why or Why not?

4. What does God being our boss cost us? (Be prepared to quote Luke 9:23–25.)

5. Read Luke 14:26. We're to "hate" our dads and moms to follow Jesus?

6. Read Mark 1:17. Do you know anyone personally in your family, neighborhood, community, church, or workplace who doesn't have a personal relationship with Jesus Christ?

7. What does a lordship disciple look like? Why?

Review the following verses:
- Psalm 82:3–4
- Joshua 1:8
- Galatians 5:22–23
- 1 Peter 4:12–19
- Matthew 6:33

- Proverbs 14:31
- Mark 1:35
- 1 Peter 3:15
- 1 John 1:19
- Matthew 28:19–28

- Psalm 1:2
- Matthew 20:25–28
- 1 Peter 3:8–12
- 1 Corinthians 16:1–2
- John 13:34–35

CULTIVATING OUR SPIRIT

➤ What do you think of Esther, Joseph (sold by his half-brothers), Rahab, Mary, Ruth, Zacchaeus, and Paul in the context of lordship, and not being perfect?

➤ Is anything or anyone hindering you from experiencing Jesus' lordship? If so, why?

➤ What do you think it would look like for you to be *legalistic* regarding lordship?

➤ Did you, while doing this lesson, ask Jesus Christ to come into your life?

➤ Recite your memory verses: Luke 6:46; 9:23–25.

BEARING FRUIT

With this thought in mind, if you are married or have a boyfriend or girlfriend, tell your spouse or significant other, that for one hour, he or she will be your lord. You will serve them (you may have to say it can't cost money or at least be reasonable and nothing related to romance). Or if you are really feeling brave, do this for your children or possibly ask an in-law or a neighbor, sports buddy, etc. You may need to reduce the time to fifteen minutes! They may ask you to clean or mow their yard—do it if you are physically able. Try as much as possible to submit without asking questions, making wisecracks, rolling eyes, complaining, or grunting. Record your thoughts and initial response of the person who becomes your lord for an hour.

Wearing God-Glasses

OUR OBJECTIVE:
Learning to consistently integrate into your lifestyle, Christ's biblical model of initiating and developing cross-cultural, economic, gender relationships, as well as learning to love people we don't like.

OUR MEMORY VERSES: 1 Samuel 16:7; 1 John 4:20–21; optional: Galatians 3:28

DAY 1

Rejection. Some, if not all of us, have experienced some form of rejection due to circumstances beyond our control. Or we have possibly rejected someone due to circumstances beyond their control. You'll be asked to revisit some possibly painful experiences. Evaluating your past actions isn't designed to judge or condemn you, but to free and heal you if need be. And it is to help you to avoid repeating any detrimental past actions that would hinder others and you.

It seems for whatever reason; some people don't like other people. Sometimes, it is because of skin color. Thus, there is tension between peoples and nations. There can be economic prejudice among people of the same culture. It can be political. Other times, it is a particular group or individual that has a bad history with another, and eventually they go to battle. Humans seem naturally to struggle with prejudice, or prejudging each other.

➤ Write in your own words what you would say *prejudging* is.

➤ Look up the word *prejudge* or *prejudice* in a dictionary. Record that definition here:

74

➤ Think of a situation where you felt you were prejudged. Jot down a few notes about what happened and why.

➤ Think of a time when you have been guilty of prejudging. Briefly outline what happened and why.

DAY 2

Believe it or not, today we will see examples of prejudging—in the Bible! Following are five examples of prejudging or prejudice. Please read each account, and record what you observe about the motivation for these judgments. Please mark these passages, as we will be revisiting these same chapters.

- Numbers 12:1–2 (In addition to looking up this passage, look up *Cushitic* or *Cushite* in a dictionary and a Bible dictionary.)
- 1 Samuel 16:1–10
- Luke 10:30–35
- John 1:43–46
- James 2:1–4

A BIBLICAL RESPONSE TO BEING PREJUDGED

Now let's look at the "conclusion" to the examples of prejudging we just viewed. This time, we'll focus on the response, result, or lesson we see in the following passages. Remembering injustices while reading these biblical responses may be difficult to process. Rather than focus on emotions, let's try to record insights we have.

- Number 12:4–13
- 1 Samuel 16:11–13
- Isaiah 11:3b
- Luke 10:36–37
- John 1:47–49
- James 2:8–9

DAY 3

Today we'll discover how to respond to difficult situations as Jesus did, if we aren't already doing so or don't know how to.

Following Jesus' steps: In John 4:4, we see how Jesus developed a relationship with someone of a different culture. See John 4:1–42. Identify as many steps as possible (some may be implied) that Jesus took to develop this relationship. During your group time, your leader will help with this section.

➤ Step 1:

➤ Step 2:

➤ Step 3:

➤ Step 4:

➤ Step 5:

➤ Step 6:

DAY 4

Ever find some people difficult to love; a family member, neighbor, co-worker, a member of your church, someone of a different culture or economic background? Well, today, we'll expose the biblical principles that can change your life if you are struggling in this area.

What is God's love like? Please read Mark 14:32–36. Zero in on the second part of verse 36. What is Jesus' response to his own will (feelings) in regards to what God wants?

➤ Read Romans 5:8.

What does it say about God's love for us? What does it say or imply about our love for God in this verse? Do we have to be followers of Christ yet?

LOVING PEOPLE WE DON'T LIKE (WHO MIGHT NOT LIKE US)

We must admit that, even as Christians, there are people we might not *like*. Including those who tend to rub us the wrong way: in-laws, church folk, co-workers, neighbors, and acquaintances. However, Christians, we are urged to *love everyone*!

Let's read the following verses. Please write the principles these passages communicate to you. And be ready in your group time to answer the question: "Is God asking or commanding us as Christians to love *everyone*?"

- Matthew 5:43–48
- Luke 6:35–36
- John 13:34–35
- John 15:12–14
- Romans 12:9–10
- Romans 13:8–10
- Ephesians 5:1–2
- 1 John 3:16
- 1 John 4:7
- 1 John 4:19–21

DAY 5

We reflect God's love through forgiving. Make a list of people with whom you have an open or ongoing conflict, including a brief description of the problem. (Don't share this list. This is confidential between Christ and you.)

➤ Read Matthew 6:14–15 and Mark 11:25.
Write down what these verses are saying to you.

Pray over your list. Ask God to help you forgive the people you identified. Pray a prayer of forgiveness for them now. Plan to pray for the people on your list on a regular basis. If you have a prayer list or journal, add their names to that now. It's difficult to continue disliking someone for whom you pray regularly.

➤ Read Romans 12:14–21.
What does this passage tell us to do for the people who hurt us?

We will find *freedom* from emotional bondage to people who have hurt us by asking God to *bless* them. This may not make sense, but it works. God's ways are higher than ours (Isaiah 55:8–9).

If we don't forgive those who have hurt us, they will continue *owning* us. Whenever you see the person who hurt you, hear his or her name, voice, etc., the hurt returns, as if the incident just happened. Any person falling into this category is, in a sense, "owned" by the other person. The person who hurt the other gains control every time the wounded person becomes aware of the one who inflicted pain in any form. This is a type of *emotional slavery*.

If we forgive the ones who have wounded us, it doesn't mean we will become best friends or even attempt that. But forgiveness is the first positive step toward our own emotional healing and freedom. We may remember the hurt; but the event's emotional grip will continue to lessen until it has no hold on us. Forgiveness lowers our stress too.

> "Each person is of ultimate worth to God, so we should be careful how we speak to people."
>
> —PAUL ANDERSEN, a disciple

We don't have to be best friends, we don't even have to like them, but we do have to love them. If you are struggling in the area of cross-cultural issues or simply want a biblical perspective on *biblical* diversity, consider reading my book, *Winning the Race to Unity: Is Racial Reconciliation Really Working?* To identify ourselves with Christ, we need to see and treat people the way Jesus did.

DEEPER ROOTS, MORE FRUIT

Memorize verses: 1 Samuel 16:7 and 1 John 4:20–21; and (optional) Galatians 3:28.

Identify an individual or a group that you're struggling to love as an authentic Christ follower, and examine why you're struggling.

HELPING HANDS

We'll begin this session about put-downs by discussing the following questions:

➤ How do you generally react and feel when you are around someone who berated someone else by telling an offensive or derogatory joke?

➤ What would be an appropriate response to someone guilty of the mistake mentioned in the previous point?

➤ When someone says something you consider offensive, what effect does this have on your attitude or disposition toward that person? Explain.

Report on your experience with last session's activity on lordship:

➤ How did it feel having a human constantly telling you what to do?

➤ How did you feel having to obey?

➤ How did you feel as you were actually doing something you didn't want to do, but had to?

➤ How did this experience influence how you feel about Jesus Christ as your Lord? Why?

GROWING TOGETHER

A crucial but sometimes overlooked aspect of discipleship is Jesus' command to *"Love one another"* (John 13:34). A part of this involves loving those we find difficult to like, loving those who have hurt us, loving those we may have hurt (regardless of our reason), and loving those who are different from us.

➤ In what ways, obvious or subtle, do you think Christians tend to prejudge or not show the love of Christ?

➤ If comfortable doing so, tell about a time you were either prejudged or were guilty of prejudging.

➤ Please read 1 Samuel 16:1–7 and 1 Corinthians 1:26–29.

➤ On what basis would Samuel have made the choice of who was to be the next king if the choice had been his alone to make? Compare and contrast this to what God looks for.

In John 4:1–42 we read about the cross-cultural encounter that Jesus had.

➤ What steps did Jesus take and how many barriers did Jesus cross in reaching out to the woman at the well?

➤ What resulted from the risks Jesus was willing to take?

➤ What barriers tend to keep us from reaching out to others who are different from us?

➤ What practical points can you take away from this? How are your God-glasses working?

"Can we really make this pilgrim journey together and, if so, at what price if it is to be made with integrity?"
—DR. WILLIAM PANNELL, former professor,
author of *The Coming Race Wars*.

You'll divide the following Scriptures within your group. Each group will read its verses and discuss what they say about our responsibility to love. After a few minutes, each group should report their insights.

- Matthew 5:43–48
- Luke 6:35–36
- John 13:34–35
- John 15:12–14
- Romans 12:9–12
- Romans 13:8–10
- Ephesians 5:1–2
- 1 John 3:16
- 1 John 4:7
- 1 John 4:19–21

LOVING PEOPLE WE DON'T LIKE

1. In Matthew 5:44–48 and Luke 6:35–36, Jesus commands us to love our enemies. As Christians, by what means are we able to do this? Explain.

2. Read Romans 12:14–21. According to these verses, what should be the standard of our conduct toward our enemies?

3. Read Matthew 6:14–15 and Mark 11:25. What role does forgiveness play in being able to love others?

4. Read John 17:20–26. What is Jesus' prayer for all Christians? Spend a couple of minutes in silent prayer. Is there anyone you are holding something against? Ask God to help you be able to forgive.

CULTIVATING OUR SPIRIT

➤ Share the memory verses: 1 Samuel 16:7; 1 John 4:20–21
➤ Share prayer requests.
➤ Ask yourself if there are changes you need to make to help you avoid prejudging people and to love people you don't like. Record the changes you identified and commit to taking action on these points.

BEARING FRUIT

Think of a friend from a different culture. Ask your friend to share with you some of his or her experiences with being prejudged. Ask questions: (How did your friend feel? How did your friend respond and why?). Take notes.

The same can apply for friends of a different gender. How did you feel when you heard the pain in their voice or saw it in their eyes?

If you possibly want to take your cross-cultural friendship to a deeper level, ask your friend how you are doing in your cross-cultural efforts (but only if you can handle the truth and won't get defensive). Let this be a learning experience for you. You are not to tell them how they are doing, unless they ask—only if they ask. If they didn't give you a good evaluation, don't hurt them because you are hurt. The point here isn't to agree, but to understand.

Share with your friend any insights or observations you have made throughout this session. If possible this week, put yourself in three situations in which you are the *other* or "out of place" person. Don't put yourself at risk. Observe how you are treated. Try to fit in. You don't have to promote your views. Try spending at least an hour in each situation. When you get home, record your experiences and how you felt.

Forgiving and Healthier Living

OUR OBJECTIVE:
Know that biblical forgiveness, unlike the world's forgiveness, is not based on emotion. Forgiveness is not a sign of weakness; to forgive will set us free from emotional slavery, depression, stress, and weakness.

OUR MEMORY VERSES: Matthew 18:21–22; Luke 17:4

DAY 1

What's *forgiveness*? Consider a dictionary definition of *forgive*. Is there a difference between your definition and the dictionary? If so, what's the difference(s)?

➤ How do you think God defines forgiveness?

➤ What does Psalm 103:12 say?

➤ What does Romans 4:3–8 say?

Consider these biblical examples of forgiveness:
- Hosea 3:1–3; of what did Hosea forgive Gomer?
- Numbers 12:1–13; of what did Moses forgive Aaron and Miriam?
- 1 Samuel 19:9–11 and 24:1–12; of what did David forgive Saul?
- Luke 10:25–37; of what did the Good Samaritan forgive the Jew?
- Luke 23:34; who does Jesus Christ forgive and of what?

➤ What is clear about forgiveness?

➤ Any different thoughts?

Forgiveness doesn't eliminate accountability or responsibility. We'll get to that later.

DAY 2

What do the following verses say to us about biblical forgiveness? Please read and record:

Mark 11:25	Ephesians 4:32
Luke 17:4	Colossians 3:13

According to Mark 11:25, the Lord Jesus *commands* forgiveness. Christians forgiving others reflects and reveals the *intimacy of relationship* with Christ. Biblical forgiveness is not a feeling or an emotion. When does God ask us to do something when we *feel* like it?

➤ How do we define *biblical love*? Consider Mark 14:32–36?

DAY 3

Are you beginning to think about some people you may need to forgive, even if they haven't asked you to forgive them? Make a confidential list of their names. And list the names of people of whom *you* need to ask for *their* forgiveness:

To help with grudges, God has created a "formula." God's forgiveness for each of us includes the following:

- Luke 6:27–31: Asking God to bless my enemy. What do I have to do?
- Philippians 4:13: Asking those that hurt me for forgiveness for *my* ungodly attitudes or actions while being mistreated.
- 1 Peter 2:21–23: How Jesus responded to mistreatment.
- Romans 12:12, 14–21: How should I respond to being mistreated?

When we refuse to forgive someone who has hurt us, every time we see them, or hear their name or voice, we lose it emotionally for a few minutes, hours, or days. If we have this type of relationship with someone, then, we are in emotional slavery. Basically, someone owns us. Ironically, often the person who has wounded us is seldom thinking about us. Yet, much of our time and energy is wasted focusing on them. Forgiving them is usually our first step to our own emotional healing. Typically, after we forgive someone, their emotional pull on us lessens. We may never forget what they did, but over time our wound will heal. And there is a tremendous difference between forgiveness and our emotional healing! Forgiveness is commanded, but emotional healing is not.

Please read Psalm 32:1–5. What application or principle can we apply or learn from this passage? The emphasis in the text is confession. But what could be an application when we consider these verses?

DAY 4

Please read Matthew 6:14–15 and 18:32–35. What do these passages teach us about God and forgiveness?

➢ What would keep you from forgiving someone?

➢ What does 2 Corinthians 2:10 say about the power of forgiveness?

➢ According to 1 Samuel 8:7, how does God respond when He is rejected by the people He created?

➢ How does Samuel eventually respond in 1 Samuel 12:19–24?

➤ If you have difficulty forgiving yourself, read Isaiah 43:18, 25. What does God command us to do in these verses?

➤ According to Romans 9:20–21, who are we really criticizing when we criticize ourselves?

The Five Languages of Apology by Gary Chapman and Jennifer Thomas, gives five ways of apologizing in the language of the person you have wounded:
1. Expressing regret: "I'm sorry."
2. Accepting responsibility: "I was wrong?"
3. Making restitution: "What can I do to make it right?"
4. Genuinely repenting: "I'll try not to do that again."
5. Requesting forgiveness: "Will you please forgive me?"

DAY 5

> "Don't let the pain of your past, punish your present, paralyze your future or pervert your purpose because you have a godly destiny."
>
> —CLARENCE SHULER

Each of us must ask ourselves what that godly destiny is. We must let go of anything hindering God's purposes in us, so we can experience that godly destiny.

Forgiving a person is one thing, but we also need to practically get over the feeling of being hurt. But how? *Letting go.*

Letting go emotionally requires intimacy with God. Intimacy with Him allows us to understand more clearly Christ's pain of rejection. His pain as He wept before going into the city of Jerusalem. Letting go releases and frees us to move.

GOMO—Get over it and move on (created by Susan Wilson, CEO of Executive Strategies). To function more effectively for God in the present, instead of constantly living in the *past* and fighting battles that God has already allowed us to win.

Forgiveness doesn't require becoming best friends. But try to treat it as though it never happened (not talking about assault, or something of that nature). For example, if someone owes you money and never pays you back, stop giving them money. But you can choose to act as if they don't owe you money.

Read Matthew 18:21 and Luke 17:4. How many times should you forgive a person? According to these verses, Christ followers are always to forgive, but it doesn't eliminate accountability, responsibility, or restitution. Forgiveness is a part of *sanctification*, which equals being made whole by God. Forgiveness leads to peace of mind. Forgiveness empowers and frees you. Forgiveness or the lack of it will have an impact on your worship of God (Mark 11:25–26).

DEEPER ROOTS, MORE FRUIT

MEMORIZE THESE VERSES: Matthew 18:21–22; Luke 17:4

➤ If you feel comfortable, share if you asked someone for forgiveness. How did it go? Were you pleasantly surprised? Why or why not? Were you disappointed? Why or why not?

HELPING HANDS

➤ "I'm sorry." "I apologize." What makes you feel that an apology is sincere? Even if the apology is sincere, but comes from someone who has really wounded you; is it difficult for you to grant forgiveness? If yes, why?

➤ Report on your experience with last session's Deeper Roots, More Fruit. Did any one in your group enter into an uncomfortable position cross-culturally? What did you do?

GROWING TOGETHER

➤ How did you define *forgiveness* before using a dictionary, or discovering God's definition? Did the dictionary definition differ from your definition?

➤ Did the biblical definition differ from your original one and the dictionary? If yes, how so?

BIBLICAL EXAMPLES OF FORGIVENESS

➤ What were some of the offenses that were forgiven? To which, if any, of the offenses can you relate?

➤ Which, if any, of these offenses shocked you, and why?

➤ Do you think you could forgive someone who is actively trying to kill you? Why or why not?

➤ How could you possibly forgive such a person?

➤ How would you define *biblical forgiveness*?

➤ What did you learn about biblical forgiveness that is different from what you previously thought?

➤ Is any part of biblical forgiveness difficult for you? If so, why do you think that is? How will you gain victory in this area?

➤ How does the fact that biblical forgiveness isn't optional make you feel and why?

➤ How does the fact that biblical forgiveness isn't emotional make you feel and why?

➤ How does the Bible's definition of love, if it does, impact the way you love and forgive?

➤ Do you hold grudges? If so, how do you forgive?

➤ How do you respond when you are mistreated?

➤ How recently have you experienced *emotional slavery*? Are you experiencing it now?

➤ Have you recently experienced freedom from *emotional slavery?* How did you get free?

➤ How are you processing the biblical concept that forgiveness is commanded, but emotional healing is not?

CONDITIONS FOR GOD FORGIVING US
➤ Does God say He won't forgive if we don't? Why?

➤ How do you feel about always forgiving someone when they repent and ask forgiveness from you? What if they don't repent?

➤ How did the passages in 1 Samuel have an impact on you and why?

➤ What is the importance of understanding and applying the biblical principle of forgiving yourself?

➤ Why do you think people struggle with forgiving themselves?

➤ How do you think God feels when we don't forgive, or appreciate ourselves?

➤ Which of *The Five Languages of Apology* is yours and why?

ACHIEVING CLOSURE
➤ How do you practically "get over" the feeling of being hurt?

➤ How can you tell you are healed?

➤ What do you think of the biblical formula for *"letting go?"* Why?

➤ Can you realistically and practically embrace Luke 17:4?

➤ What are some of the benefits of biblical forgiveness?

➤ Are you glorifying God in how you forgive? Why or why not?

➤ Are you free today, or are you in the painful chains of unforgiveness? Why or why not?

➤ If you aren't free, your freedom is only a prayer away!

CULTIVATING OUR SPIRIT

From memory, share these verses with a partner: Matthew 18:21–22, and Luke 17:4.

Share prayer requests. Be sure to include any updates to requests that you shared in the previous sessions. You should be keeping some type of prayer notebook by now to record how God is answering the prayers of your group.

BEARING FRUIT

1. If someone has asked you to grant forgiveness and you haven't, pray, contact them, and ask God to help you forgive. Note what happens.

2. If you need to ask someone to forgive you, pray, contact them (if it's safe), and ask God to help you to ask for forgiveness. Note what happens.

Regardless of whether a person grants or receives forgiveness, forgiveness doesn't eliminate accountability and responsibility. We should not pretend an offense never happened.

Growing Deeper Roots

OUR OBJECTIVE:
Disciples learn how to study the Bible for themselves and understand the difference between Bible-study and devotional times.

OUR MEMORY VERSES: 2 Timothy 3:16–17; Hebrews 4:12

DAY 1

Today, we'll discover the benefits of studying the Bible, God's personal love letter to each of us. Why study the Bible? Let's look up the following verses. For each of these, write in your own words why you want to study the Bible.

- Joshua 1:8–9
- Psalm 1:1–3
- Psalm 119:11
- Psalm 119:103–105
- Acts 17:11
- Hebrews 4:12 (memory verse)

- Ephesians 6:17
- Colossians 3:16
- 2 Timothy 2:15
- 2 Timothy 3:14–17 (vv. 16–17 are memory verses)

DAY 2

Today, we'll look at some Bible study tools. Going deeper into God's Word helps us to cultivate lasting growth and impact. As we study and find the enjoyment and value of a particular tool, we will prioritize and begin collecting resources for our personal Bible study library.

Biblegateway.com allows trial membership subscriptions that give free access to lots of Bible resources, including access to multiple Bible translations.

Church libraries and Christian colleges and universities provide a wealth of resources.

Bible software products. Research them carefully to get the best. Logos (logos.com) or biblesoft.com are excellent purchases. There are also other free tools.

Bookstores. You might ask family and friends who give you gifts to put at the top of your birthday, Christmas, and other gift lists those study resources you find best:

Bibles. The *New International Version* is a best-selling Bible. *The New Living Translation, New American Standard Version,* and the *English Standard Version* (considered the most literal translations). There is the *New King James Version,* a more conservative version. Numerous excellent study Bibles are available. A good study Bible or two is a wise investment for the serious student. Study Bibles have features such as study notes, maps, and a concordance.

Parallel Bibles include multiple translations side-by-side in one volume. To study a particular passage effectively, using more than one translation helps.

Notebook. Feel free to use a paper notebook or journal. It's also helpful to keep your Bible-study notes in a notebook or a file on your desktop or laptop. You can also keep notes on other mobile devices. Whatever works for you.

Bible dictionary. A Bible dictionary provides an alphabetical listing of biblical terms and names with their meaning and other information (such as *Unger's Bible Dictionary*).

Concordance. This contains an alphabetical list of principle words of the Bible, helping locate where and how biblical terms are used. *Strong's Exhaustive Concordance* or *Young's Analytical Concordance* are examples.

Bible Atlas. Keeping a Bible atlas nearby helps you to refer to the collection of maps that identify locations of historical events in the Bible.

Commentaries. Bible commentaries help provide the historical context (economic, political, and social), interpretation, and explanations of biblical passages.

English grammar book. Check a grammar book to help identify the various parts of speech as needed.

Dictionary. Most of us need help defining words we may not know.

Additional helps. Try Bible studies (like this one) and other books on Bible-study.

➣ Which, if any, of the other tools do you have? Which would you like to acquire in the near future and how do you look forward to using them?

Let's read and study Philippians 3:10. Try to use as many different "tools" you have or can borrow to study this verse.

DAY 3

Today, we'll discover four *methods* of Bible-study. One of the richest experiences of our Christian life is when God, through the Holy Spirit, begins to open to us the life-giving truths in His Word.

Here are four kinds of Bible study that can help any of us grow deep as it helps us explore God's Word.

Character Study:

This method begins with selecting a person in the Bible to explore—Abraham, Moses, Deborah, Joseph, David, Mary, Peter, Paul, Lydia, or whomever we would like to study. Then, we do the following:

➤ Record as much biographical info as we can compile—the individual's family history, hometown, where else he or she lived, and more.

➤ Make note of all Bible passages that relate to the individual.

➤ List the major events in the biblical person's life.

➤ List both positive and negative characteristics of this person, such as lying or being helpful.

➤ Record three things learned from studying this person's life.

➤ Look for any characteristics, positive or negative, that you might have in common with the person whom you are studying. For example, Joshua of the Old Testament was a leader of the nation, yet he was quite insecure (Joshua 1:5, 9, 18).

➤ Ask yourself what you can do to maintain or improve your positive characteristics, and what you can do to lessen or eliminate your negative characteristics.

DEVOTIONAL STUDY:

This includes reading a Bible passage and recording things that help you, such as a simple outline, basic content, the speaker, and audience.

➤ Record the key or primary idea of the passage in one sentence.

➤ Track cross-references, looking up and recording related passages.

➤ Record a personal application from this passage for your life today.

➤ *Topical Study*: Select a topic of interest, such as: faith, serving, suffering, money, love, or something else.

➤ Using a concordance, research verses relating to your topic.

➤ List *key* verses regarding the topic and summarize those in your own words.

➤ Pick out verses that have special significance to you personally; make note of why.

➤ Summarize your thoughts about the topic.

BOOK OF THE BIBLE:

➤ Choose a book of the Bible that interests you.

➤ Divide the book into sections to study: by verses, passages, outlines, and chapters.

➤ Consider using resources; for example, a commentary and a concordance.

➤ Record key themes, passages, teachings, and characters.

DAY 4

Today, we will look at another basic but foundational method for studying the Bible. This approach applies, regardless of the type of Bible study you are doing (character, devotional, topical, book of the Bible, or other).

BASIC GUIDELINES

➤ Select a plan of study and commit to it for one month; change if you find yourself needing a change of pace.

➤ Study at your own pace. Try to be consistent with your time each week. This is a Bible study, not a daily devotional. Schedule a study time, possibly at least 30 minutes to one hour. Having the same time to begin your study and same day of the week will make it easier to develop a consistent habit.

➤ Ask God to make Psalm 119:18 a reality as you study.

➤ Give the Holy Spirit permission to make changes in your life according to God's Word.

➤ Study first for personal application.

➤ Record your new commitments in your Bible study folder (computer) or paper notebook.

OBSERVE

➤ Read your Scripture passage with resources to summarize and outline as you study the text.

STEPS

➤ First: Begin by praying and reading the text, remaining open-minded, so that you may receive what God wants to teach you with a humble heart willing to obey God's Word.

➤ Second: Concentrate and observe. What is the text saying? What is its meaning?

➤ Third: Deliberately observing the text, focus on words and phrases. Ask and answer these questions: Who? What? When? Where? Why? How? The most effective way to study is to record what you observe, and what questions the text might raise for you.

Please practice these steps of observation: Study Joshua 1:8–9, recording your observation.

INTERPRET
➤ Use an accurate Bible translation(s).
➤ Ask the question: What message is this author trying to convey?
➤ Seek the context and setting by studying the verses before and after the text, and possibly the preceding and following chapters.
➤ Use Bible and English dictionaries to define unknown words. Incorporate the definitions into the text for a better understanding.
➤ Use other tools to cultivate your understanding, such as atlases, concordances, commentaries, and so on.
➤ Summarize the primary message of the text.

APPLY
➤ Now it's time for us to make personal applications. *How does this text apply to my life?* Have *I* lived, knowingly or unknowingly, in obedience to this text? What have been *my* best results and consequences?
➤ Be specific. Look for actions, attitudes, challenges, commands, examples, promises, sins, skills, talents, and warnings.
➤ Be personal. Use the personal pronouns *I*, or *me*, instead of *all Christians* or *we*. For example, begin sentences with "I need to . . ."
➤ Be practical. One example might be "I need to love my family member by cleaning the bedroom."
➤ Make goals measurable and attainable: "I need to love my spouse (or parent, or roommates) by cleaning the house this Saturday morning."
➤ Create a way you can share this new truth with a friend after you have attempted to apply the truth you have learned. This way you can share the biblical knowledge and how you felt when you attempted to apply this newly learned truth from God.

MEMORIZATION
➤ Pick the most meaningful verse or verses from the text, to memorize. If you have difficulty learning self-selected verses, consider purchasing some type of topical memory system. Check with your local Christian bookstore or online to see what resources are available.
➤ As we put God's Word in our hearts through memorization, we grow stronger and more *effective* in our Christian life. When God led Jesus to be tempted in the wilderness, He fought off Satan's attacks, quoting

Scripture. Also, we become much more effective in communicating our faith when we have many Scripture verses available to share (from experience and memory).

➤ You may want to review some practical steps for memorizing Scripture given in a previous *Challenge* session. *"My word that goes out from My mouth: It will not return to me empty"* (Isaiah 55:11).

DAY 5

Today, let's begin furthering our growth by engaging more deeply with God's Word and its relevance to us based on what we've studied this week. If you can make God's truth relevant personally, you can make it relevant to others (family, friends, classmates, co-workers, etc.).

We have the tools, and we can apply the steps of observation, interpretation, application, and memorization to Philippians 2:1–5. Consider each step carefully as you work.

DEEPER ROOTS, MORE FRUIT

While biblical *knowledge* will increase as a result of studying the Bible, the primary purpose of the Bible is to be a *life-changing* book. Consider this carefully: As good as it is to learn more about the Bible, our approach to studying God's Word should be motivated by a desire to dig deep and grow in understanding and applying His truth to life.

HELPING HANDS

We will pick one or two of the following questions to answer and share with our group.

➤ Other than the Bible, what is a book I really enjoy reading? Why?

➤ When did I first start reading the Bible on my own? Why?

➤ From the Bible, what is my favorite Bible story? Book of the Bible? Bible character? Bible passage or verse? Explain.

GROWING TOGETHER

The Word of God is indispensable to our spiritual life, as blood flowing through our physical bodies is indispensable for physical life.

➤ What is the primary reason to study the Bible?

➤ What are the benefits? In two minutes, list as many ways as you can think of (working with a partner; you'll have one person keep time while the other writes). Then, from your list of benefits, narrow it down to the top five to report to the larger group.

Divide the following verses between groups:
- Joshua 1:8–9
- Psalm 1:1–5
- Psalm 119:11
- Acts 17:11
- 2 Timothy 2:15
- 2 Timothy 3:14–17
- Hebrews 4:12

➤ Discuss what your verses say about Scripture. Specifically, for each of our passages, what is required of us in relation to Scripture and what is the subsequent benefit or reward?

➤ Who is someone who has helped you to better understand and appreciate the Bible?

➤ What Bible study tools are most helpful to you when studying God's Word?

➤ Of the four types of Bible study outlined in the personal preparation section for this session—character, devotional, topical, or book of the Bible—which is the most interesting? Why?

In the personal preparation section for this session, a method of Bible study was presented that included observation, interpretation, personal application, and memorization. Discuss what is involved in applying these components to the study of Scripture. Share from your study of Philippians 2:1–5.

1. Read James 1:23–25. What is the difference between a *hearer* of the Word and a *doer* of the Word?

2. Read Luke 4:1–13. How did Jesus use His knowledge of Scripture?

3. Now read Psalm 119:11 and 1 Peter 3:15. What other benefits are there to memorizing Scripture?

4. What is one way the Bible has influenced your life?

CULTIVATING OUR SPIRIT

➤ Share the verses from memory: John 15:7; Philippians 4:6–7
➤ Share and pray for one another.
➤ Agree on a place to meet next week before you adjourn.

BEARING FRUIT

This week's adventure is a fresh challenge to move beyond Bible reading into Bible *study*.
➤ Set a time (or times) to study the Bible this week:_____
➤ Select the place where you will study the Bible:_____
➤ Choose the type(s) of study you would like to do (see the types identified this week): _____
Applying the methods outlined, planning, and pacing will keep a growing disciple from feeling overwhelmed. Do what is most comfortable for you. Be consistent and keep in mind the ultimate goal of Bible study is to understand and apply the truth of God's Word to life.

PART 3 DISCOVERING

FOLLOWING FOREVER

SUFFERING AND SUCCESS

KEEPING TIME

KNOWING
DESTINY

Following Forever

OUR OBJECTIVE:
To understand that when God rescues us from the world, He *never* takes back and we can *never* lose our salvation.

OUR MEMORY VERSES: Ephesians 1:13–14; 4:30

DAY 1

What does the Bible say about salvation? Write down the "key words" relating to salvation in the following verses.

- Matthew 19:29
- Matthew 25:46
- John 3:15–16
- John 3:36

- John 10:28
- Romans 6:23
- 1 Timothy 1:16
- 1 John 5:11

➤ The key word repeated in all of these verses, and that describes salvation is *eternal*. What does eternal mean? Use a dictionary to get your answer. Briefly summarize your answer.

➤ If *eternal* means "forever" or "without end," how does this apply to your salvation?

DAY 2

Something happens when we become Christ followers. See Ephesians 1:13–14.

➤ What else does a person receive at salvation, besides eternal life?

These verses show that Jesus *keeps* His word (Joshua 21:45; 1 Kings 8:56).

➤ What do these two verses (Ephesians 1:13–14) tell us about the Holy Spirit?

➤ Does Ephesians 4:30 give us any additional information about the Holy Spirit?

➤ What do these verses say about the Holy Spirit?
- 2 Corinthians 1:22:
- 2 Corinthians 5:5:

➤ In your own words, define what it means to be "sealed" with the Holy Spirit.

Let's see how the word *sealed* was used when Ephesians was written.

> "In the ancient world—and it is a custom which is still followed—when a sack, or crate, or package was dispatched, it was closed with a seal, in order to guarantee that it came from the sender, and that it was intact until delivery. This was the secular use for this word in 62 A.D. The Greek word Paul used has the same meaning. It also meant *ownership, security,* and kept intact until it reached its *destination.*"
>
> —WILLIAM BARCLAY, *The Letters to the Galatians and Ephesians,*
> The Westminster Press, Philadelphia, p. 100-101

DAY 3

➤ Read Philippians 3:20.
   Where is the destination for Christians?

➤ Read 1 Corinthians 3:10–15.
   On Judgment Day, what will be judged?

Romans 8:1 says, "Therefore, there is now no condemnation for those who are in Christ Jesus." Our *works* will be *judged,* but *not us!* We may lose our rewards, but not our salvation.

➤ What does Joshua 1:9b say?

➤ What does Jesus promise in the verses listed?
- Matthew 28:20
- John 14:16–18
- Hebrews 13:5

➤ Read John 10:27–30.
  Who is speaking? Who are the sheep?

  Who would want to "snatch" them? Is that possible?

➤ Read Revelation 12:10.
  Who accuses Christians?

➤ Read Romans 8:31–39
  Who or what can separate Christians from God's love?

According to Romans 8:31–39, no one or no thing created, including ourselves, can separate us from God and His love!

➤ Read 2 Thessalonians 3:3; 1 John 5:18.
  What does God promise us in these verses?

  Titus 1:2 speaks of one of God's characteristics. What is it?

Christ's death on the cross is *timeless*. His death and resurrection reached back, cleansing the Old Testament saints (believers). Hebrews 11 provides examples of Old Testament saints' faith. Chapters 11 and 12 are connected by a conjunction. Chapter 12:1 contains the word *witnesses,* referring to Old Testament saints who are *now in heaven!*
    Jesus' death and resurrection also reaches forward, paying the penalty for the sins of future saints.

➤ Read John 17:20.
  To whom does Jesus refer?

When Christ died on the cross and rose from the dead, all the sins of us who have accepted Christ as our Lord and Savior were forgiven! Yes, we are forgiven, because of Christ's death and resurrection.

DAY 4

When receiving Christ as Lord and Savior, we experience 3 types of *sanctification*: *positional, experiential,* and *ultimate (glorification or sanctification)*. Henry C. Thiessen, in *Lectures in Systematic Theology,* speaks to these types.

Positional Sanctification eternally rescues believers from the *penalty* of sin. According to Ephesians 2:6, where are we positioned?

Positional sanctification is as complete for the youngest believer as it is for the strongest; for the mature as it is for the less-mature. It depends only on one's union with and position "in Christ." All believers are "saints" and are "sanctified" (Acts 20:32; 1 Corinthians 1:2; 6:11; Hebrews 10:10, 14; Jude v.1). 1 Corinthians proves that *imperfect* believers are *nevertheless positionally* sanctified—therefore "saints." The Corinthian Christians were *carnal* in life (see meaning in 1 Corinthians 3:1–3; 5:1–2; 6:11). Thus, this positional aspect of sanctification is *absolutely essential* if the doctrine of sanctification in its entirety is to be clearly understood.

Experiential Sanctification delivers Christians from the slavery of the *practice* of sin. We now have the ability (through the power of the Holy Spirit) to live lives free of sin (1 Corinthians 10:13). This aspect focuses on the daily walk of the Christian here on earth. We must live by faith (Romans 6:11).

Ultimate Sanctification or *Glorification* permanently removes followers of Christ from the *presence* of sin, occurring when we take our place in heaven (Revelation 21:1–8). Our faith becomes sight!

If Christ's death on the cross *is timeless,* and if the *penalty* for all our sins has been paid (past, present, and future), then what *does* happen when a Christian sins? (This is a great question! I'm glad you asked.)

➤ Read 1 Corinthians 3:10–15.
Does the believer lose his salvation? Yes or no?

What does the believer lose?

Christians who sin also suffer the consequences of their sin (2 Samuel 11—12; Galatians 6:7). For example, if a Christian couple get pregnant outside of marriage, God loves them as much as He did before the pregnancy. God will forgive each of them; but she is still pregnant. If they have the baby, there are consequences. And if they were to choose the route of abortion, there are consequences. Either choice leaves lifelong consequences (2 Peter 3:3–10).

The bottom line is that only God and the individual really know whether he or she has accepted Christ as Lord and Savior.

It has been said that if a person does not repent of every sin before dying, even though they are a Christian, they will not be saved. Well, earlier, we have already proven that the penalty for our sins is paid for *past, present,* and *future* (1 Peter 3:18—*"Christ died once for all sins"*). If we have to repent of all our sins before we die, then our salvation is based on *our works* (saying repentance) and on *us,* not God's *grace.* If we do not repent of all our sins before we die, it will affect our *rewards,* not our salvation. Use a dictionary to define *contract* and *covenant.* Write their definitions.

If one party breaks the term of the contract or covenant) then the *offended* party has the option, privilege, and the right to be released from the contract if they so desire. If the offended party chooses *not* to be released from the contract, then the contract is still *valid!* It is entirely the business of the offended party whether to remain in a contract with an *unfaithful* or *inconsistent* partner or partners.

This is exactly what God did in the covenant He had with Israel. The nation of Israel often tried to walk away from God. Israel went as far from God as it could go: worshiping gods; idol worship. Yet God *kept* His covenant. The Book of Hosea is symbolic of how Israel mistreated God and how God disciplined Israel, but He never abandoned Israel. God is honoring His covenant with believers today. So once an individual makes that commitment to God (and only God and the individual know this), then, that individual is eternally connected with God, no matter what. There's no walking away from God!

➤ Read Psalm 37:23–24.

Do these verses say God keeps us, or does He throw us away? Salvation is not based on magic words, but the attitude of our heart. God only comes to live in us if we are serious (only you and God know if you are serious).

➤ Read Hebrews 13:8.

Write it's meaning in your own words.

This verse is referring to the consistency of the essence and character of God. Therefore, God's sealing of the Holy Spirit in each believer is a continuance of the character of God revealed in the Old Testament through the New. God's grace _cannot_ be worn _down_ or worn _out!_

DAY 5

Characteristics of God: What do the following verses reveal about some of the characteristics of God? Psalms 118:1-4, 29; Hosea 3:1-4; 11:8-9; Hebrews 12:5-11; 1 John 4:19:

➤ Read Hebrews 6:4-7.

Is this passage written to non-Christians or Christians? If these verses are written to Christians, how many times can a Christian lose their salvation?

➤ Read 1 John 1:9. How often does it say that God will forgive our sins?

If, according to Hebrews 6:4-7 you can only lose your salvation _once_, does it seem that 1 John 1:9 is a contradiction? (We will cover this more in our group session.)

➤ Read 2 Peter 3:8-9. What does it say about God's patience?

➤ Read Matthew 18:21-22.

How many times does Jesus tell Peter he must forgive anyone who sins against him?

If you can only lose your salvation once, then isn't Jesus being inconsistent in telling Peter to forgive anyone 490 times? That many times really means to forgive anyone who asks _every_ time he or she asks for forgiveness.

As Christians, we cannot lose our salvation. If we could lose our salvation, we could only lose it once according to the Bible. As we have just seen, that would make God a liar (read Titus 1:2). The issue of _eternal security_ or _once saved, always saved_ should put to rest some possible fears of losing your salvation. But, it is not a license to sin. The Bible clearly explains that if

Christians sin, God will discipline (Galatians 6:7). This godly discipline always has present and eternal effects.

A logical perspective reasons that if you can lose your salvation, then you should easily be able to earn it! Here, the believer must be careful not to fall into a trick of Satan. If you can lose your salvation, then the emphasis shifts from what *Christ has done* and from what *Christ is doing* to what *you can do*! How do people become Christians according to Ephesians 2:8–9? *Earning* our salvation is eliminated by this passage. If we could earn our salvation, then Christ's death on the cross was needless!

A key word in Romans 6:23 is the word *eternal*. The definition of this word is to be without end. If we can lose our salvation, it means God would very well give us what the world might consider a *better* life; but certainly *not* the eternal one.

Read Hebrews 7:23–28. It states not only the *completeness* of Christ's earthly work, but also shows the *perfection* of His work.

PRESERVING UNITY

Christians must be careful to realize that whether someone believes in eternal security or not, it is not a biblical ground for breaking fellowship or creating division (1 Corinthians 12). As Christians, we must guard our unity in Christ. Satan is doing all he can to trick us into fighting each other, instead of us fighting together against him. His trick is to get us focused on what we can do, usually in opposition to what Christ has done, is doing, and will do.

DEEPER ROOTS, MORE FRUIT

MEMORY VERSES: Ephesians 1:13–14; Ephesians 4:30

HELPING HANDS

➤ *What, only once?* Think of some things that can only be done once, and others that are reversible? Share your ideas. Share your experience with last session's Deeper Roots, More Fruit.

GROWING TOGETHER

➤ Is God's gift of eternal life really forever? How do you define *eternal*? Why?

➤ Why do you think the Bible defines salvation as eternal life? How do you feel about your salvation being eternal? Why do you feel this way?

➤ What do Joshua 1:8–9 and Matthew 28:20 say to about how Jesus Christ and our Father God feel about you?

➤ How do these verses make you feel about Jesus Christ and God? Why?

➤ Have you ever felt alone? What was that like for you?

➤ How would you explain the concept of the Holy Spirit being sealed in you until the Day of Redemption, when Jesus returns?

➤ Do you understand Romans 8:1–2? What is being communicated to you? Do these verses allow you to disobey God without consequences?

➤ Read Hebrews 12:5–11.

➤ What happens if a Christ follower continues to disobey God? Read 1 Corinthians 3:1–15; 1 Corinthians 11:20–30; 1 Thessalonians 4:13–16.

➤ If you could lose your salvation, according to Hebrews 6:4–6, how many times could you lose it?

➤ Who is the primary entity that wants to separate us from God? Review John 10:27–30; Revelation 12:10–11a; Romans 8:31–39.

➤ Share your understanding of the three aspects of sanctification. Ephesians 2:6

➤ What is the difference between a contract and a covenant?

Whether or not we believe in eternal security has an impact on our understanding of God's grace and *legalism*. Our beliefs affect our understanding of whether salvation is about God's grace or our human effort. Our belief about eternal security affects our understanding of who's more powerful: God, Satan, or self.

CULTIVATING OUR SPIRIT

Share memory verses (Ephesians 1:13–14; 4:30) and prayer requests. Be sure to include any updates to requests that were shared in the previous sessions. You should be keeping some type of prayer notebook to record how God is answering the prayers of your group.

BEARING FRUIT

If this teaching of eternal security is new for you, consider spending some time this week reviewing this session. Ask the Holy Spirit to give you a peace about it. If you don't have a peace, don't worry about it and please don't leave the study. You've become essential to the group. If this teaching is new to you and you agree with it, ask yourself why. If this teaching is new to you and you disagree with it, ask yourself why. No matter what you believe, remember God's love for you!

➢ Do you have a friend, who is following Christ, with whom you can discuss this?

Suffering and Success

OUR OBJECTIVE:
God has purposes for everything. God often allows and uses suffering for our benefit. Suffering, spiritual maturity, and spiritual promotion seem to be linked.

OUR MEMORY VERSES: Job 2:10b; James 1:2–4 (optional: 2 Corinthians 4:15–18)

DAY 1

"My pain was preparation for my destiny."
—KIRK FRANKLIN, contemporary gospel music artist

Today, please list any frustrations or disappointments you may have with God. Be honest with yourself and God. God already knows your feelings. Such honesty is a key step to your developing transparency before God. You'll also discover how much God loves you!

➤ Have you ever been frustrated with God? Why or why not?

➤ If you are frustrated with God, was there something you think He was supposed to do for you but you think He didn't?

➤ Why do you think He didn't do it?
How do you think God feels about you? Why?

➤ Read Genesis 1:1–2:3.
When did God create man and woman? Why do you think God created man and woman last?

➤ Read Genesis 1:26–27.
We are made in "God's image." What does this mean to you?

According to Genesis 1:28, what did God do for man?

> *"You made all the delicate, inner parts of my body and knit me together in my mother's womb. Thank you for making me so wonderfully complex! Your workmanship is marvelous—how well I know it. You watched me as I was being formed in utter seclusion, as I was woven together in the dark of the womb. You saw me before I was born. Every day of my life was recorded in your book. Every moment was laid out before a single day had passed" (Psalm 139:13–16 NLT).*

➤ What has God done for you?

➤ Did you notice God *created the days for you* and not you for the days? You are special to God!

DAY 2

What does God call Old Testament believers, and New Testament *Christians*, in the following verses?

- Psalm 16:3
- Psalm 30:4
- Psalm 52:9b
- Psalm 85:8
- Psalm 145:10
- Romans 1:7
- 1 Corinthians 1:2

- 2 Corinthians 1:1
- Ephesians 1:1
- Philippians 1:1
- Colossians 1:2
- Titus 1:1
- 1 Peter 1:1
- Jude v.1

If you don't understand how much God loves you, you'll never understand or appreciate why He may allow you to suffer. What does any of this have to do with our suffering?

DAY 3

Today's assignment reveals why followers of Christ suffer and how we really feel about God.

➤ Some reasons followers of Christ may suffer: Genesis 3:1–7, and rest of the chapter. Read Romans 5:12–19. What's one reason that people suffer? See also Galatians 6:7–8.

➤ Is it ever OK to be frustrated with God? Some godly people seemed to have gotten frustrated with God. Read Jeremiah 20:7–18 and Habakkuk 1:12–13. Jeremiah and Habakkuk weren't the only ones to complain. What can you learn from their conversations with God? What did they say? And what didn't they say?

➤ Did you know most biblical leaders were reluctant leaders? Do you think God is concerned with our initial emotional response? Why or why not?

➤ So if God loves Christians so much, why does He allow us to suffer?

➤ How do you feel about God? Most people say that they love God. How do you demonstrate your love for Jesus Christ? Why do you do what you do? What is your biblical support?

➤ Do you think what you do pleases God? Is what you are doing building intimacy between God and you? Why or why not?

DAY 4

Today we'll begin to discover God's bigger picture for suffering. See if you are experiencing emotional slavery and what to do if you are.

➤ Read Joshua 1:8–9.
What kind of promise is this?

➤ Are these verses promises or commands?: Psalm 1:2; Proverb 3:5–6; Matthew 28:19–20; John 15:8;

➤ What role do you think our selfishness plays in our frustration with God while suffering—or our perception that we are suffering?

➤ What role do our "rights" play in our frustration with God while we are suffering?

➤ What if we want revenge? It belongs to God? If this happens to us, we also are still wounded and are preventing our healing. When Jesus is Lord of our lives, however, our sincere love for God has an impact on the way we view suffering.

DAY 5

Christ followers may suffer. When we read 1 Peter 1:3–9, this passage shows us another reason God allows His followers to suffer. What is it?

➤ Read Job 1:8–12 and Job 2:3–6.
Who initiates Job's suffering, and why do you think God allowed this?

➤ Read Job 2:7–10.
What is Job's response?

➤ Read Philippians 3:10; 4:11–13.
What is Paul's perspective on suffering?

➤ Read James 1:2–4, 12.
What does this passage say about why God allows Christians to suffer?

➤ First Peter 4:12–17 says what about suffering?

➤ So should followers of Christ be surprised or upset when suffering?

If we are surprised or develop a bad attitude toward our suffering or God, what are we saying about our faith? When suffering, believers should decline having a pity party. Read 1 Kings 19:9–10 and 1 Corinthians 10:13. What should you know about suffering according to these verses?

DAY 6

Today, here are some tips for us when we are suffering. One is to see God's ultimate purposes in allowing His followers to suffer.

➤ What is God's perspective on suffering according to 2 Corinthians 4:15–18?

➤ First Peter 2:21–23 says we are "called" to suffer. How do you feel about this?

➤ What do you find beneficial in Romans 12:12, 14, 17–21; 1 Peter 4:12–19?

➤ What does God promise believers in 2 Corinthians 2:14?

➤ Does God give a timetable as to when He will lead us in triumph?

➤ Write what Psalm 119:71 is saying to you:

➤ How is God speaking to you as you read 2 Corinthians 12:9?

➤ What do you think God's "Big Picture" is regarding suffering?

➤ What should we do while we are suffering? (Read Genesis 40:1–23.)

➤ What did Joseph do in the midst of his injustice?

DEEPER ROOTS, MORE FRUIT

Take some time to listen to *I'll Trust You* from gospel artist Donnie McClurkin's performance, *Live in London* (available online at Youtube.com at this writing).

"In your pain, are you helping someone else (Joseph in prison— Genesis)? Everyone is under pressure. Most of us try to act like nothing bothers us. There is a sleeping giant inside most of us. This giant is our potential for Christ—Satan doesn't want this giant to wake up. When we learn how to play with pain and perform under pressure, this is what makes a champion. Everybody . . . has pain and pressure. *Your misery is your ministry. Your suffering is your sermon. Your test is your testimony. Your pain is the power and passion of your preaching/teaching. You have been afflicted to be anointed.* God must break the alabaster box. You cannot heal what you cannot feel. Therefore, God has allowed you to be hurt so that you can pour out healing/blessings. Everything that has happened in the course of your life was not to destroy you, but to deliver you, so you can be a deliverer to other people. Therefore, regardless of your pain, *don't let the pain of your past punish your present, paralyze your future, and pervert your purpose for you have a godly destiny* (Psalm 139-13–16)! Many of our minds are stuck in rewind. Paul says, 'This one thing I do, forget what lies behind and press on. . . .' May God give you spiritual amnesia. May God give you brain damage so that you can forget the things which are holding you back as dead weight. *God wants to be a blessing to you so He can be a blessing to and through you.*"

—DR. GREENUP and DR. SHULER

111

MEMORY VERSES: Job 2:10; James 1:2–4

➤ The next time you feel you are suffering, ask God this, "What are you trying to teach me?"

➤ Review your life as a Christ follower and try to see in what areas you were better after you came through a time of suffering? If you aren't a Christ follower, evaluate your life to see if any suffering has made you a wiser person or changed the way you view and treat people?

HELPING HANDS

Report on your experience with last session's Deeper Roots, More Fruit.

➤ How did you evaluate Kirk Franklin's phrase, *"My pain was preparation for my destiny."*

GROWING TOGETHER

➤ Can you share what or who has been, or continues to be, a source of your suffering? What did you or are you doing about this situation?

➤ Do you feel God has ever been the source of your suffering? Have you ever told God about your feelings?

➤ Have you ever been the source of your suffering? Why?

➤ As you read Genesis 1:26–28, what did these verses say to you about how God feels about you?

➤ What one word does God call us in Psalm 139:13–16?

➤ What other word does God call us in Psalm 16:3; 30:4; 52:9b; 85:8; 145:10; Romans 1:7; 1 Corinthians 1:2; 2 Corinthians 1:1; Ephesians 1:1; Philippians 1:1; Colossians 1:2; Titus 1:1; 1 Peter 1:1; and Jude v.1?

➤If we don't understand how much God loves us, we'll have difficulty understanding or appreciating why He may allow us to suffer. Can you remember some reasons God allows His followers to suffer?

➤Psalm 41:9 reads, *"Even my best friend, the one I trusted completely, the one who shares my food, has turned against me."* It appears to be quite normal for godly people to be frustrated with God.

➤Read Jeremiah 20:7–20, and Habakkuk 1:12–13.
What role do you think selfishness can play in our frustration with God while suffering, or our *perception* that we are suffering? What role do our rights play in our frustration with God during suffering?

➤How do you demonstrate how you feel about God? Do you think you please God with your actions? Why or why not?

➤Are you growing closer to God? Why or why not?

SEEING GOD'S BIG PICTURE

➤Read James 1:1–18.
Some more reasons followers of Christ may suffer:
- To receive and appreciate His blessings to us (2 Corinthians 4:15–18).
- For spiritual maturity and promotion. (James 1:2–4,12). For any temptation or suffering, God has already prepared us for it (1 Corinthians 10:13 and James 1:13–15); Psalm 66:10, *"You have tested us, O God; you have purified us like silver."*
- According to 2 Corinthians 1:3–11—to comfort others
- 2 Corinthians 12:7–10
- 1 Peter 4:1–2
- Psalm 34:18–19
- Psalm 23:1, *The Lord is my shepherd;* **I have all that I need.**" NLT
- To teach us patience and strengthen our faith Psalm 28:14, *Wait patiently for the Lord. Be brave and courageous. Yes. Wait patiently for the Lord."*
- Psalm 73:21–26

- A witness to non-believers on the hope Christ followers have no matter their circumstances

When we experience suffering that isn't a result of our sin, we can be encouraged. God is about to do something amazing in our lives, which will have a positive impact on us, and those around us (believers and non-believers)!

Even if suffering is a direct consequence of our sin, God still provides and showers grace on us, even as He disciplines us.

CULTIVATING OUR SPIRIT

REVIEW MEMORY VERSES: Job 2:10b; James 1:2–4

Before prayer, share requests. Be sure to include any updates to requests that were shared in the previous sessions, including how God is answering the prayers of your group.

BEARING FRUIT

The next time you feel you are suffering, ask God this, "What are you trying to teach me?"

Review your life as a Christ follower and try to see when you were better after you came through a time of suffering. If you aren't a Christ follower, evaluate your life to see if any suffering has made you a wiser person or changed the way you view and treat people.

Keeping Time

OUR OBJECTIVE:
Disciples discover God's goals and priorities to incorporate them into life.

OUR MEMORY VERSES: Ephesians 5:15–16; Colossian 4:5–6

DAY 1

NOTE: As you begin this lesson, begin to use a journal to create schedule sheets. Or use the sheets in this book. Start to fill out the first "Schedule Sheet" for how you *actually* spend your time each week.

PRESENT SCHEDULE SHEET

Time:	Day: Sunday	Monday	Tuesday	Wednesday	Thursday	Friday	Saturday
5:00 AM							
7:00 AM							
8:00 AM							
9:00 AM							
10:00 AM							
11:00 AM							
12:00 NOON							
1:00 PM							
2:00 PM							
3:00 PM							
4:00 PM							
5:00 PM							
6:00 PM							
7:00 PM							
8:00 PM							
9:00 PM							
10:00 PM							
11:00 PM							

Review your schedule. Are you pleased with how you're managing your time? Why or why not? One of the major challenges for Christ followers may be managing our lives well. *Managing* instead of *balancing* is the preferable term because balancing implies giving all of our priorities equal weight. We should not give our family and work equal weight. Even though most of us spend more time at work than with our families, work is one way of financially supporting our family. But our family should be a priority above work.

During an evangelistic basketball trip in Brazil, a Brazilian man said to me, "In North America, computers run Americans, but in Brazil, we run the computers." His statement has a lot of truth in it. Sadly, our faith doesn't seem to have an impact on our imbalanced schedules. We may all be so busy. Do you ever wonder what God thinks about your schedule?

The woman of Proverbs 31:10–31 is often viewed as a Superwoman. Possibly a more accurate interpretation, consistent with the entire Book of Proverbs, may be to view this passage as the personification of wisdom. The thought here is that those who share godly wisdom receive favor from those who are blessed by it. It is also implied that godly wisdom produces a *well-managed* life. How can we ensure a well-managed life?

DAY 2

Goals: What are your life goals? Lack of specific life goals may result in frustration and lack of fulfillment in your life.

Priorities: Our priorities should be determined by our life goals. Things hindering or sidetracking us in reaching our life goals, shouldn't be considered as priorities.

Time: Once our life goals or priorities are determined, we must then schedule our time accordingly, so that we can achieve them.

Review: Now that our life goals, priorities (how to reach them), and time schedule are set; periodically, we will need to review and adjust when necessary. God may tweak our direction and/or we may unintentionally lose direction and/or focus.

Here are some questions you may want ask yourself or have someone ask you:

➤ What has influenced the selection of my goals, priorities, etc.?

➤ Am I reaching my goals? How can I tell? Why or why not?

➤ Is anything hindering my progress? If so, how or why?

➤ Am I getting to know Jesus Christ better? How do I know this?

➤ Who am I discipling? Who am I serving in my church? Who am I discipling in my community? Why or why not? If I am discipling or serving someone in my church, how effectively am I doing this? Is there evidence of changed lives? How can you tell?

➤ Do I grieve for people to have a personal relationship with Jesus Christ as their Savior? Is there evidence of changed lives that have accepted Christ? How can you tell? When is the last time you told someone about Jesus Christ?

Proverbs 23:7 says, "For as he thinks within himself, so he is" (NASB). So our actions reflect our beliefs. God commands us to disciple and serve people. So, we need to schedule the time we are going to spend with the people we are committed to serve.

DAY 3

Make a list of your present priorities. List them in order of importance.

1.

2.

3.

4.

Your present priorities (continued):

4.

5.

6.

7.

➤ Write the three priorities God has for your life from John 17:18–26.

➤ What things in your life need eliminating if you are going to keep God's priorities for your life?

➤ What additions does your life need if you are going to keep God's priorities for your life?

DAY 4

Scheduling
➤ What clues does God's Word give about our time management?
- Psalm 90:10–12
- Ephesians 5:15–16
- Colossians 4:5–6

DAY 5

Fill in the second "Schedule Sheet" with the priorities of your life for the next week.

➤ Write your schedule for the whole week—check it each morning for the coming day.
- List your strengths and weaknesses.
- Evaluate your ministry to others.

MEMORY VERSES: Ephesians 5:15–16; Colossians 4:5-6

PRIORITY SCHEDULE SHEET

Time:	Day: Sunday	Monday	Tuesday	Wednesday	Thursday	Friday	Saturday
5:00 AM							
7:00 AM							
8:00 AM							
9:00 AM							
10:00 AM							
11:00 AM							
12:00 NOON							
1:00 PM							
2:00 PM							
3:00 PM							
4:00 PM							
5:00 PM							
6:00 PM							
7:00 PM							
8:00 PM							
9:00 PM							
10:00 PM							
11:00 PM							

HELPING HANDS

➤ What do think of the time illustration your disciple-maker just did? Before the illustration, did you ever think there wasn't enough time in the day for you because you seem to be getting busier and busier?

➤ Now, do you think you may have enough time and need to adjust your priorities?_

➤ Report on your experience with last session's Deeper Roots, More Fruit.

GROWING TOGETHER

What do you think of the concept of *managing* yourself (if you are single), marriage/family and career instead of *balancing*? Does it make a significant difference to you, or is this simply differences in wording for the same thing? Why?

➤ Do you agree or disagree with the Brazilian comment that North Americans are run by the computer? Why or why not?

➤ Were you pleased with your present activities schedule before you did your prep work for this session? Why or why not?

➤ Do you think God is pleased with how you are using the time He has given you? Why or why not?

➤ How did reading Psalm 90:12 influence your perspective of time and your use of the time you have?

REVIEW THESE QUESTIONS:
➤ What has influenced the selection of my goals, priorities, etc.?

➤ Am I reaching my goals? How can I tell? Why or why not?

➤ Is anything hindering my progress? If so, how or why?

➤ Am I getting to know Jesus Christ better? How do I know this?

➤ *Who do you know that would enjoy taking this discipleship challenge?*

➤ Who am I discipling? Who am I serving in my church? Who am I discipling in my community? Why or why not? If I am discipling or serving some-one in my church, how effectively am I doing this? Is there evidence of changed lives? How can you tell?

➤ Do I grieve for people to have a personal relationship with Jesus Christ as their Savior? Is there evidence of changed lives for you to say they have accept Christ? How can you tell? When is the last time you told someone about Jesus Christ?

➤ What three priorities does God have for Christ followers, according to John 17:18–26?

➤ Since completing the preparation for this group time, are there any changes you need to make to your schedule? Do you need to eliminate some activities or add something to your schedule? Why?

➤ How will you live wisely among those who don't have a personal rela-tionship with Jesus Christ? How do you translate, "living wisely?" Review Colossians 4:5–6.

➤ How can you make the most of your time? Review Ephesians 5:15–16.

➤ If you are comfortable doing so, share one of your strengths and one of your weaknesses with the group?

➤ If you are comfortable doing so, share your evaluation of your service to others?

➤ When you filled out your second Schedule Sheet was it different from your first Schedule Sheet?

CULTIVATING OUR SPIRIT

Review our memory verses: Ephesians 5:15–16; Colossian 4:5–6
Before praying within your group, you'll share prayer requests. Be sure to include any updates to requests you shared in the previous sessions.

BEARING FRUIT

➣ Compare your two Schedule Sheets. Did you make any changes? Yes, or no, why?

➣ If you made changes to your schedule, in what ways was last week different for you in regards to your schedule and possibly emotional changes?

➣ Did you share with anyone about Jesus Christ last week? If so, will you please share that experience with us?

➣ Did you think about sharing, but didn't? Did you have an opportunity, but did not? If you feel comfortable, will you please share with the group?

Discovering Your Destiny

OUR OBJECTIVE:
To gain a better understanding of a disciple's identity in Christ, which will help guide us to our spiritual destiny.

OUR MEMORY VERSES: Psalm 139:16; Ephesians 2:10

DAY 1

Have you ever asked yourself why am I here or why was I born or what is my purpose in life? Most people have and they are fair questions to ask.

➣ What do you want your destiny to be and why?

➣ God created us on purpose with a purpose. Read Genesis 1:26–28, Psalm 139:13–16; Jeremiah 29:11-12; and Ephesians 2:10.

➤ Why did God create you?

➤ Read Ephesians 2:10.
As a Christ follower what does God say about your destiny?

➤ Read Psalm 139:13–16.
God is speaking through David about all of us. How do you feel God is speaking about you in this psalm?

➤ What word does the God of the universe use to describe you in Psalm 139:14?

➤ Think about this, the God of the universe calls you *marvelous* (NLT) or *wonderful* (NIV)!

➤ So no matter what anyone else says about you or names they may call you, God calls you marvelous! That is who you are!

➤ What does Psalm 139:16 say about your future?

➤ Read Jeremiah 29:11.
The context here is a promise made to the nation of Israel. What practical application can a Christ follower make from this verse, consistent with Psalm 139:16 and Ephesians 2:10?

DAY 2

The first step in discovering your destiny can be found in 2 Peter 3:9. What do you think the intent of the phrase, "He does not want anyone to be destroyed, but wants everyone to repent?"

➤ Read John 1:1–14; 3:1–17; Ephesian 2:8–9; 1 John 1:1–10.
Based on these passages, what is the first step to discovering your destiny?

➤ Read Matthew 28:19–20; 2 Timothy 2:2.
What is your general earthly purpose? Are you obeying your general earthly purpose? Why or why not?

➤ If you are not obeying your general earthly purpose, do you think this will affect your discovering your spiritual destiny? If so, why?

➤ What do you think is the second step to experiencing your destiny? Read Romans 12:4–8; 1 Corinthians 12:4–11; Romans 11:29; 1 Peter 4:10–11; Ephesians 4:11–13.

➤ What is the purpose of *spiritual gifts*? Are you using spiritual gift(s) to glorify God—how?

➤ In Ephesians 4:11-13, these are gifted individuals given to the church. How do you think Christ followers in the days of the apostle Paul discovered their spiritual gift(s)?

Today, some Christians take spiritual gift assessments or surveys. Those Christians who take these assessments determine their own spiritual gift(s). It is easy to give yourself the spiritual gift you desire. Christ followers in Paul's day didn't take surveys or spiritual assessments. Maybe they had the best method. Since our spiritual gifting is not for us, the best way to discover our spiritual gifts is serving other Christ followers and those who don't know Him. Often, they will tell what your gift is because you are serving with it.

I didn't realize that encouragement was one of my spiritual gifts until several Christ followers told me. It made sense that I didn't know it was my spiritual gift because it wasn't for me. It was for others. So they saw it before I did. Since that time, I hear it often, "You are such an encourager!"

So, your personal relationship with Jesus Christ (salvation) and your spiritual gift(s) are two steps that have an impact on your discovering your destiny.

DAY 3

This third step has already been discussed in several of the previous sessions. Review Psalm 139:13–16. What do you think this step is? Hopefully, you thought: *self-worth*. To embrace self-worth is to see yourself the way God does, which is why God calls you marvelous! A poor or negative self-image says that God is wrong about you and you are not worthy. Our self-worth can be helped or hindered by how we define ourselves.

➤ Man, who are you as a man? How do you define yourself as a man and why? Proverbs 23:7, *"For as he thinks with himself, so he is"* (NASB). Woman, who are you as a woman? How do you define yourself as a woman and why?

➤ Are you meeting your own definition of manhood or womanhood? Why or why not?

DAY 4

Fear is a common hindrance to embracing one's self-worth. Read Joshua 1:6–9, 18. What phrase is God repeating to Joshua?

➤ Why do you think God is repeating this phrase to Joshua, who has replaced Moses as the leader of the Israelites?

Fear is the enemy of faith in Jesus Christ. Fear keeps our eyes off Jesus, the God of the impossible and keeps them focused on us—and what we can't do on our own, and on our present situation.

➤ Read Galatians 5:22–23.
What is the fruit of the Spirit mentioned third? The ninth?

An essential verse to memorize is Philippians 4:13, "For I can do everything through Christ, who gives me strength." Embracing your destiny will be an act of faith! Read what Hebrews 11:6a and 12:2 say about faith and pleasing God and Jesus Christ.

DAY 5

How do you achieve your emotional balance? First is mental toughness— don't let your feelings guide your actions! Read Psalm 42:5 and Psalm 43:5. What is the psalmist struggling with? What should we do when we are struggling?

➤ What gives you peace as you think about being a man or woman? Why?

If you want to discover God's specific destiny for you, it is simple. You need to have a personal relationship with Jesus Christ. Be obedient to God's commands that you already know (read Matthew 25:14–21). Understanding and applying the truths of this Matthew passage open the door for God to promote us spiritually, based on trust and obedience.

Next, master the spiritual basics: 2 Peter 1:3–11; Psalm 119:11, 105; Mark 10:43–45; 1 Thessalonians 5:17–18. Third, make the connection as to how God Himself has gifted you (spiritual gifts). Obedient use of our spiritual gifts is linked to our spiritual destiny.

Someone said, "the victory is in the journey." God seems to use the journey to mature us spiritually. Then, because He is so gracious, He rewards us! The next step in our specific spiritual journey will be revealed after or while we're being obedient to the first three steps. Fulfillment is the result of discovering our specific purpose.

DEEPER ROOTS, MORE FRUIT

Review memory verses Psalm 139:16, and Ephesians 2:10.

HELPING HANDS

Remember when you were in kindergarten, first, or second grade? What did you want to be? Did you become what you wanted to be? Why or why not?

Do you like your present job? Why or why not? If you don't like your present job, what are you going to do about it? What is your dream job if you aren't already doing it? What are you doing to make your dream job a reality? Why or why not?

GROWING TOGETHER

➤ According to Genesis 1:26–28, Psalm 139:13–16; Jeremiah 29:11–12; and Ephesians 2:10, why did God create you? How does it make you feel to hear how the God of all creation describes you?

➤ God has a plan. Reread Jeremiah 29:11 and Psalm 139:16. What application can Christ followers make from these verses?

➤ What do you think is the first step to discovering your spiritual destiny, and why?

➤ What is the second step and why?

➤ What are the importance of spiritual gifts, and why?

➤ What is the value of obeying our general earthly purpose?

➤ Does fear or insecurity have an impact on fulfillment of purpose? What does God repeat to Joshua at least three times in Joshua chapter one? Why? What makes you fearful, insecure, or discouraged? Why?

➤ Read Psalm 42:5 and Psalm 43:5.
  With what is the psalmist struggling?

➤ In Galatians 5:22–23, what fruit of the Spirit helps us overcome fear?

The fruit of the Spirit in your life is a good indication that you are emotionally balanced.

One pastor said that, according to Psalm 42:5 and Psalm 43:5, we can talk ourselves into a negative mindset. With God's help, we can talk ourselves out of the same. In both of these verses, before the circumstance is changed, the believer begins praising God! The believer's mindset is being changed in the midst of discouraging thinking. This is what faith is all about!

➤ What gives you peace as you think about being a man or a woman? Why? How do your thoughts about yourself impact your destiny? Why?

CULTIVATING OUR SPIRIT

MEMORY VERSES: Psalm 139:16; Ephesians 2:10

Before closing in prayer, share the memory verses and then prayer requests. Be sure to include any updates to requests that were shared in the previous sessions.

BEARING FRUIT

➤ Would you evaluate yourself as emotionally balanced? Will your family and friends agree? Why or why not? Do you embrace your self-worth, that you have God's DNA—thus you are valuable—or not? Why?

➤ How do you feel about God using Joshua, who was very insecure? How do you feel about an insecure Joshua who was successful?

➤ What is your dream destiny? Are you living it? Are you in process? If not, why?

➤ How are you doing telling others about Jesus Christ?

PART 4 **RELATING**

BEING SINGLE AND CONTENT

DATING MR. OR MRS. RIGHT

BUILDING
RELATIONSHIPS
THAT LAST

Being Single and Content

OUR OBJECTIVE:

For the single disciple (high school, college, young adult, never been married, widow, or divorcee) to learn to appreciate his or her present relationship status. This requires learning to trust God for his or her present and future relationships. For the single disciple to understand his or her self-worth to God, to others, and to himself/herself in the context of his/her present social situation.

OUR MEMORY VERSES: Philippians 4:12; Proverbs 3:5–6

DAY 1

Know who you are.

> "If you are not content being single, you won't be content married."
>
> REV. HERB BRISBANE

If you are a Christ follower and single, you are *complete!* You don't have to date or be married to be complete before God. So please don't feel that you are abnormal because you aren't in a relationship or aren't married. Don't feel pressured because well-intentioned family members, friends, or church members keep asking you why you aren't married. It is not most people's intention to be insensitive. *Do not rush into a relationship!* What does 1 Corinthians 7:1 say about being single? The term *man* here includes women.

➤ Reserve at least 10 minutes or more to write down your strengths as you see them. Then, ask people who love you like your immediate family members and a close friend individually what are your strengths and only a close friend. If you don't have a close friend, that is okay-nothing is wrong with you. Write them down. Look at them and process them. Thank God for your strengths and how He has made you.

➤ Take another 10 minutes or more and write down your weaknesses. Be careful here because we often are too critical of ourselves. Next, ask people who love you such as your immediate family and close friend if you have one about your weaknesses. None of us are perfect, so all of us have weaknesses, some we can change and some we can't. This may be difficult to hear. We don't want to become defensive however.

Thank God for making you aware of any new weakness.

➤ Do you remember Genesis 1:26-28 from one of our first sessions? Reread those verses.

➤ What is God saying about you?

Do you realize in whose image you are made? Because you are made in God's image, you have value—you are important. So whether or not you are in a relationship, you bring something to the table. Focus on your value (self-worth) Thank God that He made you unique!

DAY 2

What does 1 Corinthians 7:1 say about being single? The term "man" here includes women.

➤ What does 1 Corinthians 7:8–9 say about being single?

➤ What is the only reason the Apostle Paul tells singles to marry?

➤ Summarize 1 Corinthians 7:17–24:

➤ According to 1 Corinthians 7:24, could God be calling you to be single for this time or possibly forever? What are verses 25–28 of 1 Corinthians 7 saying to you?

The "present crisis or distress" refers to the persecution of Christians without any protection from the government. So Paul is telling singles that it may be easier to endure this difficult time without the additional concerns for a spouse and/or children.

➤ Respond to 1 Corinthians 7:32–38:
Remember 1 Corinthians 7:28. So you aren't sinning being single or married. The key is being in God's will. Paul felt a person can do more for God if the person is single.

DAY 3

God uses single people.

➤ Read Genesis 37:1.
How old was Joseph when God was interacting with him?

➤ Read Genesis 39:6–9.
When Joseph was still single and tempted by Potiphar's wife, what did Joseph say to this tempter?

➤ Read Genesis 41:41–45.
Joseph remained faithful to God while single and years later, what happened to Joseph?

Some may view singleness as an injustice, but see Joseph's perspective— on the injustice he received at the hands of his half-brothers.

➤ Read Genesis 50:15–21.
When did God first speak to Samuel, according to 1 Samuel 3:3–10? Is Samuel a boy, teenager, or a man?

Saul and Samson were single when called by God. Even though they didn't live a consistent life for God, God still used them to glorify Himself.

➤ When did God call David, according to 1 Samuel 16:1–13?

God worked through Rahab (Joshua 2). We don't know if Lydia was married or not, but God used her (Acts 16).

We know God certainly used Paul. Some say that Paul's position with the Pharisees and other religious organizations required marriage. Others question whether Paul was married and his wife left him after he became a believer.

DAY 4

What did Paul command Timothy to do (1 Timothy 4:12)? What do you think Paul referred to when he mentioned the word *purity*?

➤ Paul commanded Timothy (possibly 30 and single) to do what in 2 Timothy 2:22?

➤ To whom does your body belong, according to 1 Corinthians 6:18–20?

➤ Why do you think verse 18 commands us to flee sexual immorality? What do you think are the consequences of disobeying this command from God?

Please understand, a decision to marry or remain single should come from God.

A statement God gave me when I was in graduate school, after I had seriously injured my knee: God spoke to my heart and mind, "My best for you is right now! It was not yesterday, nor is it tomorrow. My best for you is right now!" That helped me so much when I felt helpless. These words from God helped me learn to stay in the moment or at least look for God's blessings in my present situation instead of wishing it away for a better day. How does this apply to you in your singleness?

➤ What does Lamentations 3:22–23 say to you?

We don't want to miss out on God's blessings today by wishing for yesterday or dreaming of tomorrow, hoping for better circumstances.

DAY 5

What did Paul say about being content (Philippians 4:11-13)? It seems that the level of our intimacy with Christ and understanding of our self-worth have much to do with our contentment regardless of our relationship status.

I also believe living out our life dream is another key element. Do you have a life dream? If so, write it out. Are you living it or making progress to it? If not, why? Your answer to this question usually reveals whether you are content or not. If you aren't making steps to live out your dream, why is that? Don't let fear hold you back. We'll discuss fear later.

To experience contentment, make sure you have fun at least weekly, daily is better and it lowers stress. Laugh, even at yourself sometime.

Having some independence is another element of contentment. If you are single let one of your goals be to support yourself with parental assistance. And if all possible, don't live at home.

If you do live at home, insist on paying some kind of rent. Initiate helping around the house—cooking, cleaning the kitchen and taking out the trash for example. If you live at home, be an asset and not an overgrown teenager. Don't let your parents be your "fail-safe." If you do, it will retard your growth. If you desire to marry, this lack of maturity will impact who is attracted to you and who you will marry. Immaturity attracts immaturity and maturity attracts maturity.

Living on your own helps you mature. It allows you to get to know yourself better as you learn to deal with all aspects of live on your own.

Write yourself a love letter today, reminding yourself of the truths about being single that you've considered this week. You can make it a rhyme or rap or fill the line of a notebook page or a journal.

DEEPER ROOTS, MORE FRUIT

MEMORY VERSES: Philippians 4:12; Proverbs 3:5–6
Consider this blog: www.SingleRoots.com

HELPING HANDS

➤ How does your family treat you as a single individual, especially during holidays? How do you feel about this?

➤ If you attend church, how do church attendees and the pastoral staff treat you as a single person? How do you feel about this?

➤ How does the world treat singles? How do you feel about this?

➤ How does the treatment you receive affect your self-worth?

➤ How does knowing that God loves you make you feel? Do you feel if God really loved you, that you would be in a relationship? Do you ever feel God is punishing you because you are single?

GROWING TOGETHER

SINGLE, EQUAL, BLESSED, AND COMPLETE!

➤ What do you think of Herb Brisbane's statement: "If you are not content being single, you won't be content married"?

➤ How do you process the following paragraph?

> Know who you are: If you are a Christian and single, you are *complete*. You don't have to date or be married to be complete before God. So please don't feel that you are abnormal because you aren't in a relationship or aren't married. Don't feel pressured because well-intended family members, friends, or church members keep asking you why you aren't married. It is not the intention of most to be insensitive. *Do not rush into a relationship!*

➤ Why does Paul urge singles to remain single as he is in 1 Corinthians 7:8–9; 25–28?

➤ In 1 Corinthians 7:24, Paul refers to being single as a calling? What do you think of that?

➤ Respond to 1 Corinthians 7:32–38.

GOD USES SINGLE PEOPLE.

➤ How old do you think Joseph was when God called him (read Genesis 37:1)?

➤ When being tempted by Potiphar's wife, what does Joseph say to her (Genesis 39:6–9)?

➤ Joseph's faithfulness, while single, to God was rewarded how and when (Genesis 41:41--45)?

➤ What does Paul command Timothy, who is approximately 30 years old and single, to do in 2 Timothy 2:21–23? What do you think about sexual purity until marriage? Why?

➤ According to 1 Corinthians 6:18–20, to whom does your body belong? Why?

➤ How does Genesis 50:15–21 help you deal with your singleness?

➤ Who are other singles God used in the Bible?

➤ According to Lamentations 3:22–23, how does your faith help in the context of being single?

Below are two phrases to help you understand Lamentations 3:22–23 and live your single life, embracing your self-worth, and living by faith in God's plan for you.
- "God's Best for me is *always right now*, not yesterday and not tomorrow!"
- You have a *godly destiny*, so don't wish your time away on tomorrow or wanting things to be different. Learn to embrace today!"

CULTIVATING OUR SPIRIT

- Being single and content—really?
- How can you make this happen?

MEMORY VERSES: Philippians 4:12; Proverbs 3:5–6

Before praying within your group, you'll share prayer requests. Be sure to include any updates to requests you shared in the previous sessions. You should be keeping some type of prayer notebook by now to record how God is answering the prayers of your group.

BEARING FRUIT

Process the following statements by yourself or with family and friends this week. Be ready to share your thoughts during your group session.

Some reasons you may be single and they aren't bad: You may not be emotionally ready, which may cause you to be dependent and needy, creating a co-dependent, dysfunctional, and ultimately destructive relationship. The person God wants to connect you with isn't ready or you aren't ready. Why are you defining yourself by your relationship status? Another reason for singleness may be a broken heart that hasn't healed

God doesn't want to compete for our affection with anyone. There could be spiritual lessons God wants you to learn before allowing you to be in a relationship. God may be allowing you to see whom or what you love most—Him or being in a relationship. Maybe God wants you to determine if you will continue living for Him if you never get into a relationship. Maybe God wants you to understand *that life's ultimate goal isn't getting married*, it is a personal relationship with Him.

Maybe singlehood is also a time to get to know God personally and individually before being in a relationship. Getting to know God better would also allow you to get to know yourself even better, as well as who will be a tremendous match for you! More reasons can be found. Check out this single's book,: *Single and Free to Be Me.*

Dating Mr. or Mrs. Right

OUR OBJECTIVE:
For the single disciple whose pre-marriage culture dates and desires to marry, to prayerfully consider asking *time-tested* and *life-changing* questions of the potential spouse. These questions will assist disciples in their efforts to find a relationship that glorifies God, one that is mutually beneficial to the disciple and the potential spouse. These questions do not guarantee future happiness but *may* help the disciple avoid an unnecessary and painful relationship.

OUR MEMORY VERSES: Matthew 6:33; 2 Corinthians 6:14

DAY 1

Remember, if you have a personal relationship with Jesus Christ, you are complete and don't have to have a boyfriend or girlfriend, or a spouse! So don't rush into a relationship and then have to rush out! Let God guide you into a relationship.

Please don't feel any pressure or that you are abnormal because you are not in a relationship, nor do you have a desire to be in a relationship. Process this statement before trying to complete this lesson!: If you do want to be married, focus on being the right person more than finding the right person because God won't bring His Best to mess!

Questions you should consider answering before dating:

➤ Read Philippians 4:11–13.
In the context of relationships, what is this passage saying or implying about you and relationships? Why do you think it is saying this?

➤ Read 1 Corinthians 7:7.
If you don't care to date, why is this? There is nothing wrong with feeling this way.

➤ Why do you want to date? What do you want to accomplish when you date?

➤ Are you going to kiss on your first or second date? Why or why not?

➤ What attracts you to the opposite sex? Why? (body, personality, etc.?)

➤ What criteria do you use when determining whether to continue or end a relationship?

➤ How much does the physical aspect play in your dating relationship?

138

➤ Based on your biblical knowledge (provide scripture supporting your view), what role should the physical play in your relationship?

➤ What does the Bible say about kissing?

➤ How about hugging?

➤ What about touching your date's body?

➤ What is OK and what is crossing the line?

➤ Does Ephesians 5:3 say anything about the physical?

"Another observation I have made about premarital sex is that often it leads to unhealthy marriages. This is because the *one-flesh relationship* has begun prematurely. Frequently, couples who have already begun a sexual relationship come to me for premarital counseling. For both partners, when the sexual relationship has started, the *soul relationship* has been forged. So, they work hard to make the relationship succeed and deny the signals that might be telling them not to marry. Because they are already heavily invested, they plunge headlong into a marriage that should never take place.

"You see, in the New Testament, the words *adultery* and *fornication* are basically interchangeable. The original language of the New Testament was Greek. The Greek words that are translated *adultery* and *fornication* refer to a concept that basically means 'illicit sexual relationship.' The only sexual relationship given to us by God is the relationship between husband and wife. Within these boundaries, sex is intended to be a beautiful, joyful expression of love and commitment. Everything else is illicit and violates scriptural principles."

—*The Dance of Restoration: Rebuilding Marriage After Infidelity,*
ABEL ORTEGA AND MELODIE FLEMING

DAY 2

God won't bless relationships that violate His principles. In the context of dating, what principles could apply from Colossians 3:23–24?

➤ What does 1 John 1:9 say about God?

➤ Do you consult God about your dating? If yes, when do you consult God about your dating?

➤ Are there any biblical guidelines for dating? If yes, what are they? 2 Corinthians 6:14 reveals what possible safeguard or principle for Christian dating?

➤ Ephesians 5:22–25 is written for married couples, but what are at least two applications singles can practice from this passage (you may need to ask your leader for help with this question)?

➤ Hebrews 13:5 teaches us what characteristic to avoid in a potential spouse?

➤ Do you pray on your dates? Why or why not?

➤ Is there a possible danger in praying with the person you're dating?

➤ Do you share your *faith story* (testimony) on your first date? Why or why not?

➤ Why should you?

➤ What should hearing your date's faith story (testimony) confirm for you?

➤ What 4 elements should you hear in a faith story (testimony)?

➤ Do you have a godly couple who checks out all your dates (to whom you are accountable)?

➤ If you are dating a high school graduate, then answer these questions:

➤ Does the person you're dating live at home? Have they ever lived away from home on their own?

➤ How do they handle money? Are they in debt? Do they have a viable plan for eliminating their debt?

➤ Are they a saver or spender (not a right or wrong answer—just an observation)? Which are you?

➤ Do both of you tithe (look it up if you don't know what it means) to your local church?

➤ First Corinthians 16:1–2 says what about financially supporting your church?

DAY 3

Do you have a spiritual foundation/support group: a group of people praying for your future spouse (is it God's will for you to get married)?

➤ Is your church praying for all the singles? If not, why?

➤ Ladies, talk to me about being *submissive*. What does it mean to you?

➤ The word "submit" biblically means a "voluntary yielding." So there is no dictatorship in marriage.

➤ Men, talk to me about being *servant- leaders* (the head). Define this term in your own words.

➤ So why do you want to get married? What will marriage do for you besides legalizing sex?

➤ Will dating/being married enhance your relationship with God? How?

➤ Will dating/being married make you a better follower of Christ? Why or How?

➤ How will you feel about God if He says He doesn't want you to date or get married?

➤ Will you still love God?

➤ How do you feel being single at church?

➤ How does the church treat you as a single?

➤ If you are single and have children, should this affect your dating? If so, how?

DAY 4
A biblical perspective on dating: Genesis 24

FINDING MR. OR MRS. RIGHT:
➤ v. 3,4—*Principle of Commonality* (2 Corinthians 6:14)
➤ v. 12–15, 26–27, 52—*Principle of Prayer* (prayed before meeting girl, prayed once he met her and continued to pray)
➤ v. 15—*Principle of Timing* (may be right person, but is it the right time?— Brenda and me)
➤ v. 16—*Principle of Beauty* (potential spouse needs to be beautiful to *you!*
➤ v. 16—*Principle of Virginity* (1 John 1:9: *2nd Virginity*; Ephesians 4:15, 25) (University of Minnesota and Administration of Children and Family stats reveal pre-marital sex's impact on lasting marriages, reduces chances of lasting marriages to 15 percent!)
➤ v. 18—*Principle of Character* (servant: vs.18,19-watering 10 camels—each camel can drink 20 gallons=200 gallons!)
➤ vv. 1–9, 28–52—*Principle of Parental Consent* (not required, but best to get parents' blessings if they love you—they can often see critical issues we can't because we're in *love!*)
➤ v. 67—*Principle of God's Will* (Information from Dr. Gary Chapman's book, *The Marriage You Always Wanted.*)

➤ How does Philippians 4:6–7 apply to dating or wanting to be married?

➤ Is there a difference between "worrying" and being "concerned?"

➤ Read Psalm 139:13–16.
Remember how God feels about you.

➤ How does Matthew 6:33 impact your dating or trying to find someone to date and/or marry?

One of my favorite phrases I share with singles is this one (please know I was 31 before I got married):
Don't seek to find God's best; concentrate on being God's best. God's not going to send His best to mess!

DAY 5

Spiritual checklist to lead you toward being God's best:
- Spiritual growth
- A personal relationship with Jesus Christ as Savior and Lord
- Quiet Time (devotional—time alone with Christ—Mark 1:35)
- Prayer—talking and listening to God—John 10:16b
- Bible study—2 Timothy 2:15
- Spiritual Gift(s)—knowing what your gift is and using it
- Biblical priorities—time management
- Evangelizing—sharing your faith in Christ with others
- Discipleship—spiritual reproduction
- Commitment to church—time, gifts, financial

Review our MEMORY VERSES: Matthew 6:33; 2 Corinthians 6:14

This session is an excerpt from Building Lasting Relationship's *Christian Dating* Seminar. BLR conducts this seminar for high school, college, and the marketplace (never married and divorcees). Visit www.clarenceshuler.com for more information about BLR's seminar or to book him for one.

HELPING HANDS

Your leader has a special game for you. Please follow his or her directions.

➤ How did you feel about this game? Did it provide any clarity for you in regards to relationships? If so, please share with the group.

GROWING TOGETHER

If these three statements are true, what impact do they have on you and how you feel about your present relationship status? Why?

TRUTH: "If you have a personal relationship with Jesus Christ, you are complete! You don't have to have a boyfriend, girlfriend, or a spouse to be complete! So, don't rush into a relationship because you might have to rush out of it! Let God guide you, whether you should be in a relationship, when, and with who."

TRUTH: "Please don't feel any pressure or that you are abnormal because you are not in a relationship. Neither are you abnormal if you have no desire to be in a relationship."

TRUTH: "If you do want to be married, focus on being the right person more than finding the right person because God won't bring His Best to mess!"

➤ According to Philippians 4:11–13, what should be our attitude toward ourselves and God, regardless of our relationship status? Why?

➤ How do you feel about what Paul says about marriage in 1 Corinthians 7:7?

Answers you should have before going out on a date
➤ As you completed the days of individual study before this group session, how did you feel about all the questions about dating?

➤ Which of these questions did you find most helpful? Why? Which one was the most intriguing to you and why?

➤ What role do you think the physical should play in dating relationships? Why?

➤ What for you is "crossing the line" physically? Read Ephesians 5:3. God considers sex before marriage immoral. Review two paragraphs from *The Dance of Restoration: Rebuilding Marriage After Infidelity,* Abel Ortega and Melodie Fleming, pgs. 9–10.

GETTING TO KNOW YOUR DATE AND LETTING THEM KNOW YOU

➤ Do you share your faith story on your first date? Why or why not?

➤ Will you pray with your date and at the end of your date, and not just over the food? Why or why not?

➤ Should you ask if your date is a Christ follower? Why or why not?

➤ If your date says he or she is a Christ follower, how should you respond? Why?

➤ In your prep for this group session, you read Dr. Gary Chapman's principles taken from Genesis 24 for a prospective mate. Review them. Do you agree or disagree with this list? Would you add anything to this list? If so, what and why?

A RELATIONSHIP SUPPORT GROUP

➤ Read Proverbs 11:14.

A relationship support group are people who love you enough to tell you what you don't want to hear, but need to hear. You listen to them because they love you. Consider having a relationship support group. You probably have one in the form of your family and/or close friends. If you don't, maybe you can develop some friends at church or in your community. And you can always ask God to provide a group for you. It can be one or two people. You don't need a lot of people for this kind of support.

> "Don't focus on trying to find God's best. Focus on being God's best because God's not going to send His best to mess."
> —CLARENCE SHULER

145

CULTIVATING OUR SPIRIT

MEMORY VERSES: Matthew 6:33; 2 Corinthians 6:14

Before praying within your group, you'll share prayer requests. Be sure to include any updates to requests you shared in the previous sessions in your prayer notebook.

BEARING FRUIT

➤ Evaluate your dating habits. Do you think God is pleased with them? Why or why not?

➤ If you have a support group, have a time with them to evaluate your dating practices. Listen to their input and be honest with yourself. Do you need to make any changes? If so, why?

Consider that, even if you don't marry the person you are dating, he or she should be more like Christ for having dated *you*. And you should have helped to prepare this person for whomever he or she marries. If you were wounded by someone, can you forgive them without an agenda to restore the relationship? You may want to review sessions, *Wearing God-glasses and Forgiving and Healthier Living.*

➤ If you're not interested in being in a relationship that is fine. Why don't you want to be in a relationship? Did you ever hurt someone in a previous relationship? If it was your fault, is it possible to ask that person for forgiveness?

Growing a Relationship That Lasts

OUR OBJECTIVE:
For the single disciple, to see what is required in a biblical marriage.

For the married disciple, to experience the marriage God has always wanted them to have, by incorporating biblical principles. It is incorrect and sad for a Christian to believe they can have a right relationship with Christ, yet simultaneously mistreat a spouse.

OUR MEMORY VERSE: Ephesians 5:33

DAY 1

God has a purpose for marriage. Read Genesis 2:18. What does God say about man (humans) being alone?

➤ Marriage seems to be God's desire for most people, but there are some exceptions. What does 1 Corinthians 7:7–9 say about marriage and being single?

So it seems that it isn't God's will for everyone to be married. So if you're single, don't feel abnormal. Don't rush into marriage to simply escape being single, loneliness, or boredom.

In Genesis 2:18, the word "Helper" is mentioned as another name for woman.

➤ Read Psalm 33:20, Psalm 70:5, Psalm 115:9. and John 14:16 (NASB)
To whom does the word "Helper" refer in these verses?

Since we understand that the term "Helper" in the Bible is usually another name for God or the Holy Spirit, whether you're a woman or man, we can't ever think of this term as inferior.

➤ From reading Genesis 2:22–25, what do you think is God's primary purpose for marriage?

GOD'S OTHER PURPOSES FOR MARRIAGE:
● Genesis 1:26–27
● Genesis 1:28
● Genesis 18:18

GOD'S PRIORITY OF MARRIAGE:
➤ Read Deuteronomy 20:7.
What priority does God place on marriage?

➤ In 1 Timothy 3:2–4, who is mentioned first, the wife or the children?

➤ According to 1 Timothy 3:5, how can a church leader be disqualified from leadership?

Whether you are a church leader or not, God's biblical priority is God first, spouse second (even if this is a remarriage and you have children from previous marriage), children third, and then your job or ministry. Getting this out of order is a certainty for disaster, even if this is a remarriage that includes children from a previous marriage.

➤ In Ephesians 5:22–6:4, who is mentioned first, the wife or the children?

DAY 2

Growing together spiritually:

➤ What principles in Philippians 2:1–5 are crucial in developing spiritual intimacy with your spouse?

➤ According to Ephesians 5:21, what should spouses do for each other?

When the Bible was first written, there were no chapters and verses. So, often in most translations, Ephesians 5:21 isn't grouped with the verses following it; but in the context of marriage, it probably should be.

➤ Use a dictionary and a Bible dictionary if you have one to define "submit."

➤ In Ephesians 5:21–33, what is the wife's responsibility to God?

➤ According to these same verses, what is the wife's responsibility to her husband?

➤ In verses 21–24, what is the husband's responsibility to his wife?

➤ In this passage (vs. 21–33), what is the husband's responsibility to his wife?

➤ Ephesians 5:33 says the wife needs what from her husband? What does this verse say the husband needs from his wife?

148

Verse 33, commands each spouse to fulfill the other's need. Remember, biblical love is an action, not an emotion!

➤ What does 1 Timothy 5:8 say to men about providing for their families?

This verse says men are to especially provide for their immediate family (they come first). Remember, this includes the wife first and children second.

➤ Hebrews 13:5 says our perspective of money should be what?

DAY 3

Correctly handling conflict can lead to intimacy. Few if any marriages are conflict-free. And the goal of a marriage glorifying God isn't to be conflict-free, but how the couple resolves their conflicts. Conflicts are natural, simply because men and women are different; not superior or inferior, just different. Our family backgrounds and previous relationships, whether dating, engagements, or previous marriages, all impact our marriages. So "fighting" or conflict is inevitable. But, conflict, correctly and effectively handled, can actually increase a couples' intimacy.

> "Conflict is reality for most couples, so not having conflict is not reality for most couples. So avoiding conflict is attempting to avoid reality." —FAMILYLIFE MARRIAGE CONFERENCE

> "A goal of effective communication is listening carefully and expressing yourself carefully." —FAMILYLIFE TODAY

There is *never* a place in marriage for verbal or physical abuse.

Typically, when a couple has conflict, one spouse has offended the other. Let's look at what *FamilyLife Today* calls the "anatomy of anger":

• A partner's offense
• Which leads to a hurt
• If hurt isn't healed, it leads to anger (If this anger isn't controlled, usually nothing is resolved. Uncontrolled anger may be experienced by leaving the room, yelling, shutting down, etc.)

- If this anger is controlled (it should resemble a yellow "Caution" light that something is wrong. It is the responsibility of the fiancée/spouse who has been hurt to inform their spouse that they have been hurt). Mind reading is overrated and often wrong. Please don't say to your spouse "If you loved me you'd…" But if this anger is controlled, it opens the door to reconciliation
- During this reconciliation you can have:
- Forgiveness
- And resolving the issue (sometimes) resolving the issues come first
- This opens the door to transparency, which is what attracted you to each other to begin with
- And then intimacy because now, you have learned one more thing about your spouse than you knew before. Knowing this new information and *applying it*, makes you closer than you were before the conflict.

Maybe a question that should be considered is, "Why do you get angry?

James 1:19 has two essential tips for handling conflict which are:
- Remembering our lessons on forgiveness and
- Letting go will also be helpful.

WHY DO YOU GET ANGRY?
➤ Bob Horner says *"The measure of a man or a woman is what it takes to make him or her mad."* He also says, *"The maddest people are the saddest people."* Is it a sin to be angry according to Ephesians 4:26?

➤ How does Ephesians 4:15 say we are to speak the truth?

➤ Ephesians 4:29 tell us how to "speak the truth in love" by:

➤ What is the purpose of "speaking the truth in love" according to Ephesians 4:29?

➤ Galatians 6:1 tutors us in how to "speak the truth in love" by:

➤ Ephesians 4:32 and Colossians 3:13 give us the motive we need to forgive because:

➤ According to Matthew 5:23–24, how important is forgiveness to worship?

Recovery and counseling circles have used this tool for decades.
Hunger
Anger
Lonely
Tired
All of the above can contribute to conflict.

What do you do if your spouse says after you ask for forgiveness, "I can't forgive you right now." Then ask your spouse, "When can you forgive me? (Don't quote Luke 17:4 at your spouse). This question is based on the principle of Ephesians 4:26. My wife and I encourage couples to not go more than 48 hours maximum without forgiving their spouse. Usually in a marriage, one spouse tends to be more emotional than the other (it isn't always the woman). This allows one spouse time to process the issue emotionally. And it assures the other spouse that the issue will be discussed.

If the couple has children, the children will or will not learn how to forgive based on what they see their parent do. The Administration of Children and Families' research indicates that marriages impact families to the third and fourth generation.

PROCESSING BIBLICAL RECONCILIATION:
Take action—what changes do you need to make in how you respond to conflict? Consider speaking with your spouse about it. Listen to his/her response. Don't fight or get defensive, but pray together about it. Hold hands if possible. Prayerfully consider asking the question, "What can we do to make our marriage all we want it to be?"

➤ Proverbs 15:4 says what about the influence of our tongue?

DAY 4

Sexual intimacy

"A covenant involves the exchange of seals or signs. In two separate ceremonies, the bride and groom exchange signs or seals as part of their covenant. First, is a public ceremony; they give rings to

one another as a sign of the vows they have made. Later, they seal their covenant vows through the joining of their bodies in a private ceremony. Sex not only is part of the covenant of marriage, sex is the divine seal."

—TIM ALAN GARDNER, *Sacred Sex: A Spiritual Celebration of Oneness in Marriage*

Research states most wives want their husbands to hug them 10 to 12 times a day in a non-sexual way (guys, don't count aloud). If the only time men touch their wives is to have sex, then, many wives often feel simply like sex objectives.

First Corinthians 7:2–4 recommends that a husband and wife should have sex on a regular basis. The couple needs to agree and compromise as to what works best for them. The focus on this passage is serving and giving, not demanding. When is the only time a couple should abstain from having sex as stated in 1 Corinthians 7:5?

➤ This verse implies that couples should also do what together?

➤ In the early years of their marriage, what did Isaac do for his wife, Rebekah? (Genesis 24:67; 25:21a)?

➤ Pastor Alvin Simpkins, former director of prayer for Promise Keepers says, "If a man doesn't pray for his wife, he doesn't love her!" What does 1 Peter 3:7 say to men about prayer and their wives?

➤ Sexual Intimacy is also for pleasure. Read Song of Solomon 1:2. How can love be compared to wine?

➤ Read Hebrews 13:4.
What two things does this verse say about sex in the context of marriage?

➤ What are some romantic tips we can glean from Song of Solomon 5:10–16 and 7:1–9?

➤ Proverbs 5:19 commands us to do what?

DAY 5

What does God say about divorce? First of all, I'm not condemning or judging anyone who has been divorced. Few have not been impacted by divorce in some fashion. Without desiring or intending to offend anyone, let's see what God says about divorce in Malachi 2:13–16?

God makes at least three crucial statements in this passage. Notice: God says He, "Hates divorce!" He doesn't hate divorced people, huge difference! Don't believe Satan's lie about this!

➤ What is Matthew 5:31 saying about divorce?

➤ Matthew 19:1–9 says what about divorce?

➤ Now read 1 Corinthians 7:10–11's statement about divorce and separation. What does this passage say?

People often ask me about divorcing if their spouse is beating them or if there are drugs involved. This Corinthian passage says couples can separate. I never tell people to stay or leave. I have seen God restore marriages in both situations. A biblical Christian can be invaluable. Just because people say they are Christian counselors, doesn't make it so. Ask them about their salvation experience. Check their references. If they aren't using the Bible in their counseling, lose them!

One method that dramatically lowers the issues above is pre-marital counseling. The Administration of Children and Families and some Christian marriage organizations say that for couples who have pre-marital counseling, it increases their chances of a successful marriage by 75 percent! These same researchers have discovered that pre-marital sex drastically lowers a couple's chances for a successful marriage! So from the verses above, what appear to be the only two biblical grounds for a biblical divorce?

People, even Christians, often tell me, "God wants me to be happy and I'm not happy with my present spouse." I tell them God wants them to be "holy" and if they are "holy" they are often happy. But God really wants us to be obedient!

If we put tremendous effort (prayer, pre-marital counseling, accountable to those who love us, faithful to biblical principles, have the peace of the Holy Spirit, and don't violate our conscience) before our marriage, there is an excellent chance to build a marriage that will last and be mutually fulfilling! The more committed you are, the more compatible you'll be.

> "The issue isn't compatibility, but commitment."
>
> –GREG SPECK

➤ How does Hosea respond to his adulterous wife? This is grace! This is the heart of God; grace and forgiveness.

➤ Ladies, you hear all the time how the man is the head, but 1 Peter 3:1-6 allows you to be the neck to turn the head. How so?

DEEPER ROOTS, MORE FRUIT

MEMORY VERSE: Ephesians 5:33

HELPING HANDS

Relationships can make you shout for joy or cry!

➤ Think back to elementary school, did you have a boyfriend or girlfriend? How did that happen? What attracted you back then to your former significant other? What ended the relationship?

➤ Have some of you been the dump-er in a relationship? How did you feel? Have some of you been the dump-ee? How did you feel?

➤ With your relationship experience, what would you say is the key to building a lasting relationship? What is a key to destroying a relationship?

CULTIVATING OUR SPIRIT

➤ Report on your experiences with last session's Deeper Roots section.

GROWING TOGETHER

You can have the marriage you have always wanted!

➢ What is God's purpose for marriage according to Genesis 2:18? Why?

➢ If God is so pro-marriage, how do you respond to 1 Corinthians 7:7–9?

➢ After working through the preparation for this group time, how do you feel about the word *helper*.

➢ Does God have any other purposes for marriage?

A God-honoring marriage has God first, spouse second, the children third, and then, career or ministry (1 Timothy 3:3–4). The husband-wife, dad-mom relationship gives the children security, even in a blended marriage. Couples who put the children before the marriage often have spoiled, uncontrollable children. And this couple often divorces after the children leave home. Frequently, by putting the children first, the couple grows apart. The same is true for children in a blended situation.

➢ In marriage, who comes first, the spouse or the children? Why?

➢ What about in a blended marriage?

➢ How are your spouse and you growing together spiritually? A key to building a marriage to last is Philippians 2:1–5. What is the key action for a spouse (making an application)?

➢ According to Ephesians 5:21–33, what is the wife's responsibility to her husband and what is the husband's responsibility to his wife?

FIGHTING FAIR!
● In the context of marriage or dating, when fighting is referred to, it is not physical!

155

- There is no place in relationships, dating or marriage, for emotional, verbal, or physical abuse!

➤ What were some of your takeaways from prep section in regards to conflict? Any you can share with the group? You may need to ask your spouse first.

➤ Is anger a sin?

➤ What is speaking the truth in love?

➤ What is wrong with "I'll forgive you when I feel better about what you said or did"?

God created sex! Response to this statement: To have great sex, you need to connect with your spouse (not the person you're dating-no sex for you) emotionally, intellectually, and spiritually. The physical act of sex that God intended is a celebration of these three connections.

➤ Since God is a God of love, why does He hate divorce? Remember, He doesn't hate divorced people.

➤ What do you think of the verses regarding divorce in the prep section?

➤ Why do you think God hates divorce?

➤ Do you think God hates divorced people? Why or why not?

➤ What do you think of Hosea and Gomer?

➤ What do you think of the two following statements?

> "The issue isn't compatibility, but commitment."
> —GREG SPECK

> "The more committed you are, the more compatible you'll be."
> —CLARENCE SHULER

➤Women, you hear all the time how the man is the head, but 1 Peter 3:1–6 allows you to influence the head. How?

BEARING FRUIT

MEMORY VERSE: Ephesians 5:33

Before praying within your group, you'll share prayer requests. Be sure to include any updates to requests you shared in the previous sessions and share how God is answering the prayers of your group.

Please take some time to review the list of Marriage Resources on page 235. I have found these titles to be invaluable to making your marriage all that God wants it to be.

Marriages are similar to cars in that they need regular tune-ups.
I strongly recommend attending a marriage retreat/seminar yearly!

PART 5 MODELING

MANAGING MONEY

KNOWING OUR ENEMY

USING TECHNOLOGY

FEARING AND
FAITH

Managing Money

OUR OBJECTIVE:

Presenting the disciple with God's view of money and stewardship. Several Bible teachers have said that Christ mentioned money more than 3,000 times. If that's true, understanding God's perspective and use of money is critical for disciples desiring to glorify Christ in this crucial area of his or her life.

OUR MEMORY VERSES: 2 Corinthians 9:7–8

DAY 1

Define *stewardship* in your own words. Then use a dictionary to define: Christian personal giving:

- 1 Corinthians 16:1–2
- 2 Corinthians 9:6–7
- Romans 15:25–27
- Hebrews 6:10

MONEY'S IMPACT

Marriage counselors believe money is the *number two or three* reason couples divorce.

Author and teacher Gordon MacDonald commenting on the North American Church, reports, "One of the greatest missing teachings in the American church . . . is the reminder to men and women that nothing we have belongs to us."

Randy Alcorn writes in *Money, Possessions and Eternity*, "Only 15 percent of pastors say they have been equipped by their denomination or seminary to teach biblical financial principles. Only 2—4 percent of seminaries offer courses, seminars, or Bible studies to teach stewardship principles, and only 1—2 percent of Christian colleges offer such training."

"If a person gets his attitude toward money straight, it will help straighten out almost every other area in his life," Billy Graham counseled. He continued, "Give me five minutes with a person's checkbook, and I will tell you where his or her heart is."

DAY 2

There is a biblical view of money and stewardship. Read and summarize Genesis 1:4, 10, 12, 18, 21, 25, 31.

➤ Read and summarize Genesis 1:26–28; 2:7–9

➤ Read and summarize Gen 12:2–7; 13:1–8; 24:35; 32:13–16; 41:57

➤ Read and summarize Exodus 11:2–3

➤ Read and summarize Exodus 25:1–9

➤ Read and summarize Exodus 36:2–7

➤ Read and summarize Leviticus 25:23; cf. Psalm 24:1

➤ Read and summarize Exodus 23:10–11; Deuteronomy 15:1–18

➤ Read and summarize Exodus 22:25–27; Leviticus 25:35–37; Deuteronomy 23:19–20

DAY 3

Can we determine the amount of an Old Testament *tithe*?

➤ Read Leviticus 27:30–33; Numbers 18:8–32; Deuteronomy 14:22–29. What happens if you redeem your tithe? Leviticus 27:31.

➤ Read and summarize Leviticus 5:7, 11; 12:8; 14:21–22.

➤ Read and summarize Leviticus 19:9–10; Deuteronomy 24:19–22; Ruth 2:1–7.

➤ Read and summarize Proverbs 21:13; Proverbs 29:7

➤ What is the biblical view of debt? Proverbs 22:7

Author and teacher Andy Stanley asserts, "When you begin to view your wealth from God's perspective, you'll see that the thing to fear isn't giving away too much, but sowing too little." (From *Fields of Gold: A Place Beyond Your Deepest Fears, A Prize Beyond Your Wildest Imagination*)

DAY 4

What does the Bible say about *stewardship*?

➤ Summarize Matthew 18:23–35.

➤ Now define *stewardship* according to Luke 10:25–37.

➤ Summarize Luke 12:13–21.

➤ Summarize Matthew 6:25–34, Luke 12:22–32.

➤ What's your definition of *treasure*?

➤ Summarize Matthew 6:19–21, Luke 12:33–34.

➤ Who do you serve? Summarize Matthew 6:24, Luke 16:13–15 cf. Mark 8:36.

➤ What do others say about stewardship?

> "HEART
> **H**e owns it all.
> **E**very day is an opportunity.
> **A**ction is required.
> **R**emember your blessings.
> **T**hank Him.
> Move from success to significance, from wealth to generosity, from achievement to service, and from status to relationships."
> — KEN BLANCHARD and S. TRUETT CATHY,
> in *The Generosity Factor*

> "There are three conversions necessary: the conversion of the heart, mind, and the purse."
> — MARTIN Luther

> "The key to understanding God's will in finances is to have the proper understanding of stewardship. A steward is one who man-

162

ages another's property. We are merely stewards of God's property while we are on earth. He can choose to entrust us with as much or as little as He desires, but in no case will we ever take ownership. Quite often, the demonstration of our stewardship is not how much we give, but how we react when there is much to give. We cannot experience peace in the area of finances until we have surrendered total control of this area to God and have accepted the role of steward."

— *THE WORD ON FINANCES* by Larry Burkett

"Stewardship is the act of organizing your life so that God can spend you."

—LYNN A. MILLER

"I do not believe one can settle how much we ought to give. I am afraid the only safe rule is to give more than we can spare. In other words, if our expenditure on comforts, luxuries, amusements, etc., is up to the standard common among those with the same income as our own, we are probably giving away too little. If our charities do not at all pinch or hamper us, I should say they are too small. There ought to be things we should like to do and cannot do because our charitable expenditures excludes them."

—C.S. LEWIS

"He who has God and everything has no more than he who has God alone."

—C.S. LEWIS

DAY 5

What you have learned about God's perspective regarding money, based on the biblical verses you have read in this lesson, and quotes by the various individuals?

➤ If you are in debt, what is your plan to get out of debt?

DEEPER ROOTS, MORE FRUIT

➤ Will what you have learned change the way you manage the money God is allowing you to steward? If so, how? If not, why not?

➤ Are you financially supporting any Christian ministries other than your church? If no, would you like too? If you would like to, and you are not, what is keeping you from giving more?

MEMORIZE these verses: 2 Corinthians 9:7–8

HELPING HANDS

➤ You have just received an unexpected $5,000. What will you do with it? Why?

GROWING TOGETHER

➤ Is it you money, my money, God's money?

➤ Did your definition of stewardship differ from the dictionary? If so, how?

➤ In the section of preparation for this group time entitled *Christian Personal Giving*, what were your first impressions? Will this section influence you in the future in giving to others?

➤ Do you, or people you know, struggle with managing their money? If so, why do you think that is?

➤ Do you have a savings account? If you have debt, do you have a working, systematic plan to lower it consistently and as quickly as possible? Do you have an emergency fund? What are you doing regarding your retirement? (You don't have to share your answers aloud.)

➤ What does the Bible say about retirement?

➤ What is God's view of money and stewardship?

➤ What is God's perspective about the poor? What does God command Christ followers to do about the poor? Why do you think God feels this way?

➤ Are you financially supporting the church you attend, if you go to church? Why or why not?

➤ What is a *tithe*? How many tithes were there in the Old Testament?

➤ What should be our treasure? What is your treasure? Why?

➤ Are you financially supporting any Christian ministries other than your church? If no, would you like to? If you would like to and you are not, what is keeping you from giving more?

CULTIVATING OUR SPIRIT

MEMORY VERSES: 2 Corinthians 9:7–8

Before praying within your group, you'll share prayer requests. Be sure to include any updates to requests you shared in the previous sessions. You should continue to keep some type of notebook record of how God is answering the prayers of your group.

BEARING FRUIT

Do you have a budget? If you have never done a budget for yourself, take time this week to do it. See exactly how much money you make and how you are spending it.

➤ Would you consider yourself a *spender* or *saver*? There is no condemnation here, this is how most people are wired and fall into one or the other category.

➢ What was your biggest takeaway from this session on money? Why?

➢ Did this session change the way you view money? If so, why?

➢ Did the session change the way you budget or spend money? If so, how?

➢ How do you describe the way God feels about the poor? How has God's view about the poor had an impact on you?

Knowing Our Enemy

OUR OBJECTIVE:
For the disciple to be aware of his enemy, Satan, and the enemy's goal and strategies. The disciple must learn how to cultivate use of God's Word, and embrace the Holy Spirit's indwelling guidance, to resist Satan.

OUR MEMORY VERSES: 1 Peter 5:8–9; 1 John 4:4

DAY 1

Satan hates God and all Christ followers. He is our enemy. Don't be alarmed. One of Satan's most effective tools is *fear*. Read 1 John 4:4 before pondering today's questions and comments.

THE WAR ZONE
➤ Read Ephesians 6:12.
Where are some of the evil forces located?

➤ Read Daniel 10:1–14.
What is going on with Daniel and the answer to his prayer?

➤ Read Job 1:6; 2:1–2.
Where is Satan when he is talking to God? Where had Satan been?

➤ Read Isaiah 14:12; Ephesians 2:2; and Revelation 12:9.
Where is Satan's domain?

➤ Read Revelation 20:7–10.
What ultimately becomes of Satan?

DAY 2

Today, you'll discover the different names of our enemy. For the following Scriptures, identify the various names (you may want to consult several Bible versions).

- Genesis 3:4
- Matthew 12:24
- Matthew 13:19
- Luke 10:18
- John 8:44
- John 14:30
- 2 Corinthians 4:4

- 2 Corinthians 6:15
- 2 Corinthians 11:14
- Ephesians 2:2
- 1 Thessalonians 3:5
- Revelation 9:11
- Revelation 12:10
- Revelation 20:2

DAY 3

Here we see how Satan came to be and some of his characteristics.

- Isaiah 14:12–14
- Ezekiel 28:14–17

- Revelations 12:7–9

CHARACTERISTICS

For the following verses, record characteristics of Satan you identify (some implied):

- Genesis 3:1–4
- Job 1:6–11
- John 8:44
- 2 Corinthians 11:3

- 2 Corinthians 11:14
- Ephesians 2:2
- 1 Timothy 3:6–7
- 1 Peter 5:8–9

DAY 4

Satan can be powerful. But he isn't all-powerful; God is! Look up these verses, writing in your own words what they say to you about Satan's power.

- Matthew 25:41
- Luke 22:3–4
- John 8:42–44
- Acts 13:8–10

- 2 Corinthians 4:3–4
- Ephesians 2:1–3
- 2 Thessalonians 2:9–10a
- 1 John 3:10

ATTACK TACTICS SATAN USES

Look up the following Scripture passages and record the tactics you identify.

- Genesis 3:1
- 1 Chronicles 21:1
- Job 2:7
- Zechariah 3:1

- Matthew 4:5–6
- Matthew 4:8–9
- Luke 22:31
- 2 Corinthians 11:3

DAY 5

Satan attempts to deceive followers of Christ.

DECEPTIONS

1. You should be able to do miracles on demand.
2. You receive power in words through spells and witchcraft.
3. Seek personal experiences of demonic influence, out-of-body experiences, visions, and hearing audible "voices."
4. You can become a god.
5. Faith equals sight.
6. Seek wealth, health, and power.
7. You can have heaven here on earth.
8. You can accomplish great things with Satan's help.

SATAN MAXIMIZES	GOD EMPHASIZES
the temporal	the eternal
immediate pleasure	long-term rewards
momentary feeling	lasting effect
having fun now.	the cost, later!

God's power to overcome Satan; read these verses, noting the power God gives His followers.

- Psalm 119:11 and 105
- Matthew 18:18–20
- John 14:12–14
- 1 Corinthians 10:13
- 2 Corinthians 2:10–11
- Ephesians 6:10–18

- 2 Thessalonians 3:2–3
- James 4:7–8a
- 1 Peter 5:8–9
- 1 John 2:12–14
- Revelation 12:10–11

DEEPER ROOTS, MORE FRUIT

➤ Read Acts 19:13–16.
What can happen to those trying to find demons to cast out? Christians don't chase the devil. When God wants us to have an encounter, He will have spiritually prepared us for such an encounter. The devil or demons may come to you, but only if they have received permission from God (see Job 1:12; 2:4–7; Mark 5:1–13; Luke 22:31).

MEMORIZE THESE VERSES: 1 Peter 5:8–9 and 1 John 4:4.

HELPING HANDS

Let's reminisce about our school days. Choose one or two of the following questions to answer and share with the group.

➤ When was a time you were picked on or harassed by a bully? Describe the circumstances.

➤ If there was a bully in your life, what things did you do to try to keep the bully from bothering you? Were you successful?

➤ What common characteristics do you think bullies share?

➤ Were you a bully? If so, why?

➤ What advice would you give a child who's dealing with a schoolyard bully?

GROWING TOGETHER

We're not going to dwell on Satan and his power. Rather, we'll focus on our awareness of our enemy and the power we have through Jesus Christ. We don't need to fear Satan, but we should have a healthy respect for and awareness of his evil tactics. Christ has won the war; we don't need to lose unnecessary battles.

THE BATTLE, OUR ENEMY, HIS NAMES, LIMITS, TACTICS, LOCATIONS

➤ When you hear the phrase *spiritual warfare*, what thoughts or images come to mind?

➤ According to Ephesians 6:10–12, who is our struggle against? How would you classify the kind of struggle we are in? What are the stakes?

➤ Read Deuteronomy 18:9–13.
What additional forms do practices like these take today? Why should such activities be avoided?

➤ In the following passages, what are the names given to Satan?
- John 14:28–31
- 2 Corinthians 11:14
- 1 Thessalonians 3:5
- Revelation 12:10

How do these names reflect on his character and the roles he tries to play in our lives?

➤ Read the following passages, noting the limitations of Satan's power.
- Mark 5:1–13
- Acts 13:6–12
- Ephesians 2:1–4
- 1 John 4:4

How powerful is Satan? How is his power limited?

➤ Read the following passages, noting Satan's strategy for doing evil in the world.
- Genesis 3:1 and 2 Corinthians 11:3
- Job 2:7 and Luke 22:31
- Zechariah 3:1
- Matthew 4:5–7

What tactics do you think Satan finds especially effective in your community? Why?

➤ Read the following passages, noting where Satan goes to do evil.
- Job 1:7; 2:1–2
- Ephesians 2:1–2
- Ephesians 6:12
- 1 Peter 5:8–9

What are specific ways you see Satan active in the world?

DEFEATING SATAN THROUGH CHRIST'S POWER

Read the following passages, noting how in Jesus we can find help confronting Satan's evil.

- 1 Corinthians 10:13
- Matthew 17:21
- 2 Corinthians 2:10–11
- Ephesians 6:10–18
- Mark 9:17–29
- 2 Corinthians 10:3–5
- 1 Corinthians 6:7
- 1 Timothy 1:18
- 1 John 5:14–15
- Matthew 18:18–20

➤ What weapons are available to us in our spiritual battle? Which of these are offensive weapons? Defensive weapons? What are practical ways we can use these tools?

➤ In regards to the means available to us to resist or overcome Satan, what resource do you appreciate the most? Why?

➤ Read Matthew 4:1–11.
How did Satan attack Jesus? How did Jesus rebuff Satan's attacks? How can we apply this tactic?

➤ Read Acts 19:13–16.
What lessons about engaging in a spiritual battle do you see in this passage? Explain.

CULTIVATING OUR SPIRIT

Report on your experience with last session's Deeper Roots, More Fruit.

Share memory verses: 1 Peter 5:8–9; 1 John 4:4.

Before praying within your group, you'll share prayer requests. Be sure to include any updates to requests you shared in the previous sessions.

BEARING FRUIT

➤ Record anything new you learned from last week's session. Did you learn anything new about yourself?

➤ Has your exposure to this session changed your view of prayer or the way you pray? If so, how, and why?

➤ How do you feel about Satan now? Are you more aware of his strategy? If yes, how so?

➤ Do you have another Christ follower in the group or outside of the group to discuss the impact of this session with?

➤ If you attend a church, when is the last time you heard a sermon about Satan or spiritual warfare? If it has been more than a year or two, why do you think that is?

You and your Bible can make an Internet exploratory trip to browse DVDs, visiting the horror section. You're not on sites to rent; you're there to pray. Aren't there a lot of horror movies? Our culture has a fascination with the "paranormal" and an almost tragic misunderstanding of Satan and evil. Some videos present Satan as an all-powerful being; others, as an almost comic figure. As you discovered in this week's study, both representations are lies.

Satan is not all-powerful. In fact, his total defeat is assured through the power of God. But Satan is also not a pitchfork-carrying horned caricature. He's real and so is spiritual warfare.

Leave the horror section. Open your Bible and read Romans 8:31–39. How does reading this make you feel now? Read this passage again. How much does God love you? How powerful is the God who loves you? How far can Satan separate you from God? How secure are you in God's love?

Over the course of your regular activities, be sensitive to spiritual battle that's going on all around you. When you run across the things of Satan, stop and pray.

Using Technology

OUR OBJECTIVE:
To learn the privileges, responsibilities, and practices for technology use in relationship with others in a way that glorifies God.

OUR MEMORY VERSES: Colossians 1:16; 3:23–24

DAY 1

Read what Colossians 1:16 tells us about the context of humanity's technological advancements and why. What are some of the ways technology benefits you and most people?

➤ Why do you think God would allow us to make so many amazing technological advancements?

➤ What are some of the advances of technology in the last five years?

➤ Do you think people are too dependent on technology? If so, how? And if you say yes, why? Do you think people should be more dependent on technology?

➤ Read Ecclesiastes 1:9.
Are you able to reconcile this verse with the continuing technological advances of today?

DAY 2

Once upon a time, we only communicated by the spoken word, the written word, and the telephone. Today, many, if not most, communicate through the Internet. For example, email, Instagram, Twitter, Facebook, Snapchat, and the next development. We also communicate with our cell phones, especially texting.

➤ Read Colossians 3:23–24.
What do these verses say about our motive in all we do?

➤ Would you say technology has improved or hindered our face-to-face communication with each other? Yes or no and why?

Technology has helped us become more productive in the workplace through the Internet, email, and texts for brief, factual communication, as well as delivering information more quickly. Due to constant connection to technology, we need to be aware of a tendency for some to work more than they intended because of easy access. These unintentional habits take time away from significant others, spouses and families. Could this possibly happen to you? Or are you already experiencing this? If so, how can you either avoid it or if you are already working more than you intended, how can you correct this?

Read 1 Timothy 3:4–5. This passage lists requirements for church leadership. One requirement is managing your family well; do your children obey you and have proper respect for you? What do you think is necessary for this to happen? An increasing number of successful secular companies are embracing this biblical principle because they are learning that our personal lives and relationships away from the office (success at home) overflow to success at work.

If we apply this biblical principle, what should our priority be; our family, our ministry, or our career and why? Read Ephesians 5:21. If you're in a relationship or are married, what is your responsibility to your significant other or spouse regarding work?

DAY 3

What is Colossians 4:6 saying to us about *relationships* **and** *technology*? How can you do this?

➤ How is technology good for relationships and why?

➤ Can technology negatively impact relationships and how?

➤ It seems technology has changed the way relationships develop. This isn't necessarily good or bad. Technology, such as Skype, can tremendously help long distance relationships. Texting can be great for quick, short updates. But, can technology unintentionally interfere with the closeness of the relationship? If so, how?

DAY 4

➤ **What does Romans 14:22–23 say about being morally right,** responsibility, and being sensitive?

➤ Have you ever been wounded by way of technology? How so?

➤ Did you ever discover you had unintentionally wounded someone through technology? How were you made aware of it?

What are some examples of technology abuse? I received the email below from a close friend. It is a very complimentary email, but initially, I was offended. We love each other and nothing will change that. But we had to work through this email. Read it and see why I may have been offended.

> "Okay, truth time. I've been reading your Twitter thoughts and I know that you are posting them as part of promoting your book. It's a good idea. However, for some reason, they are coming across as shallow to my heart. I know you to be deep bit [but] I don't see that heart in these posts. When other people that come across this way, I normally stop following their posts. I won't do that with you, however, because I care too much. I'll keep reading but pray about digging deeper. God has a lot to say through you! :) Folks need meat and you have a ton of that in your amazing heart! Know I love and care for you, deeply! Have a blessed weekend!"

Whether you agree I should have been offended or not, if you can find a reason why, write it out. Why I got offended (not saying I was right to be offended):
- My love language is "words of affirmation and encouragement."
- Resented that my tweets were called shallow.
- Didn't want to write tweets worrying about if they met my friend's standard of being "deep."
- And my friend didn't provide an example of what "deep" looked like.

➤ What could have been a way for my friend to have communicated with me? If so, how?

I would have preferred a phone call asking me, "What is your purpose for tweeting? This would have allowed me to explain that I'm just trying to connect, share truth, but not be "deep" in most of my tweets, but have people think. And it may have kept my friend from offending me by understanding my motive for what I was doing. And think how much time was wasted on this! A phone call would have been so much quicker.

Perhaps emails and texts aren't the best way to communicate emotional and complicated issues. We also need to understand that what is not emotional for us, may be emotional for the person who receives our email or text. Even though we may be best friends, we seldom know each other as well as we think we do. Emotional technological communications can easily be misinterpreted. Satan will attempt to cause people to misinterpret them.

Emotional issues need face-to-face interaction, where you can see facial expression and body language. If face-to-face isn't possible, then, at least a phone call to hear voice tones is helpful.

Some people feel they get to know others better through technology because they are more open to write how they feel than deal with someone face-to-face. But is this really helping or is it a false security because some people will write what they would never say in person?

If a person can't or won't confront someone face-to-face, is this saying anything about that person's character or integrity?

➤ Read Matthew 18:15–16.
How does this verse relate to dealing with a misunderstanding?

DAY 5

As much as we have personalized our technological communications, it is still impersonal.

➤ Read Colossians 3:22–23 and 4:6.
Emails and texts don't have voice inflection, so they can be easily misunderstood.

TECHNOLOGICAL ABUSES:
- Cyberbullying
- Sexting
- Improper emails, text, Facebook posts, chats, tweets, etc.
- Forwarding damaging emails

● Being impersonal, not thinking or caring about who you are offending. We can't imagine or anticipate the pain we may cause someone.

➤ Where, or how, have you seen these kinds of communications? How does this happen?

➤ Who is most vulnerable?

➤ Is there anything you can do about it? Why or why not?

As much as I love technology, I'm concerned that we are losing some of our social skills in communicating effectively face to face, which is so much quicker and more efficient. It takes less time to complete a discussion than constantly texting back and forth.

TIPS FOR TECHNOLOGICAL COMMUNICATION:
➤ Give facts, get to the point, be brief.
➤ Emails and texts—if not sure about sending them, don't send them (Romans 14:22–23).
➤ Don't respond to emotional emails or texts with an email or text, and don't respond right away—cool off, pray, seek wise biblical counsel.
➤ Be careful of "You" emails. Instead, use "I think" or "from my perspective" language.

We are not saying that technology is bad or evil, yet, with all its benefits, we must be responsible and accountable for how we use this tremendous gift. Below is a worst-case scenario of technology misuse, which speaks to face-to-face communication:

Former Rutgers student Dharun Ravi said he wasn't responsible for Tyler Clementi's death. Speaking out a day after, Ravi said he did not cause his gay roommate to commit suicide. He said that what he learned during the trial convinced him he was not responsible for Clementi jumping to his death from the George Washington Bridge on September 22, 2010, three days after a snooping incident.

According to the television program about the tragedy, Dharun and Tyler, who were roommates, were having problems with each other. but didn't talk verbally to each other. They only communicated with each other by texting. "In this digital world, we need to teach our youngsters that their actions have consequences, that their words have real power to hurt or to help," Tyler's mother, Jane Clementi, resolved. "They must be encouraged to choose to build people up and not tear them down."

➤ What does Ephesians 4:29 say?

HELPING HANDS

➤ How do you feel about technology and why? Think of inventions that have improved life over the last 100 years. Share them with the group.

➤ Were there any downsides to those inventions that improved the overall quality of life for most people? Share with the group.

➤ If you love technology, please tell why.

➤ If you don't love technology, please tell why.

Report on your experiences with last session's Deeper Roots, More Fruit.

GROWING TOGETHER

➤ Read Colossians 1:16.
What perspective does this verse give you in regards to humanity's technological advancements and why?

➤ Why do you think God has allowed so many technological inventions?

➤ Are people too dependent on technology? Why?

➤ Do you believe technology has a positive or negative impact on our faith?

➤ How do you process Ecclesiastes 1:9 in the context of todays technological advances?

➤ Are you getting what I'm saying?

➤ Have you experienced misunderstandings via social media? How did you discover there had been a miscommunication? Were there any consequences?

➤ Would you say that technology has improved or hindered face-to-face communication? Yes or no, why?

TECHNOLOGY AND QUALITY OF LIFE

Technology is amazing. It can help us do more things more easily and quicker. Therefore, in theory, we should be able to work less and be more productive. Working less should equate to more time with our loved ones.

➤ Is this your experience with your work and time with your loved ones? Why or why not?

➤ Read 1 Timothy 3:4–5.
What do you think the phrasing "manage household well" means here?

➤ What more does the Bible show Christ followers about communicating through social media? Read Romans 14:22-23 and Galatians 5:22–34.

➤ Review Dharun Ravi and his roommate, Tyler Clementi's, story. Did you learn anything from their communication? If so, what?

CULTIVATING OUR SPIRIT

Revisit our memory verses: Colossians 1:16; 3:23–24

Before praying within your group, you'll share prayer requests. Be sure to include any updates to requests you shared in the previous sessions. Consider the record of how God is answering the prayers of your group.

BEARING FRUIT

Try to honestly evaluate how you use technology.

➤ Ask people who love you enough to tell you what you might not want to hear, but need to hear, about their perspective on technology and you.

➤ Is there anyone whom you have unintentionally offended through social media? Will you consider calling them and asking for a meeting to apologize?

Is there anyone who offended you via social media? Will you consider calling them and asking for a meeting to discuss the matter? This person may or may not apologize. Don't get mad if he or she doesn't apologize. At least you shared your perspective (graciously). And who knows, that person may apologize later. If they don't, this will help you evaluate your relationship with that person. Also, take into consideration whether the person is a Christ follower or not.

Fearing and Faith

OUR OBJECTIVE:
For disciples to understand that he or she may never completely eradicate fear from his or her life, but have victory over any fear through Jesus Christ. And to learn that fear is often the first tool Satan uses to get Christ followers' eyes off Jesus, focusing only on circumstances.

OUR MEMORY VERSES: Joshua 1:8–9; 2 Timothy 1:7

DAY 1
How do you define *fear*?

➤ Read Joshua 1:8–9.
What does this verse say to you about fear and you? What is or are your fears and why?

We're often told our fears are irrational: "Why would you fear that?" Of course, another person may say this because of their fear, or being unable to help you.

➤ What do you do when you are fearful now? What did you do when you were fearful as a child?

➤ Did someone do something bad to you when you were a child? You don't have to share who and what it was. But you can if you feel safe with this group.

➤ What were some things that made you fearful as a child? Why?

➤ Read Genesis 3:6–9.
Why were Adam and Eve fearful of God?

➤ Read 1 Samuel 17:1–11.
Who was afraid of Goliath?

Our fear can be the consequence of our own actions or due to forces beyond our control.

DAY 2
What does 1 John 4:18 communicate about fear?

➤ Read Genesis 12:10–12.
Who is fearful and what is the cause? Who created this circumstance?

➤ Read Genesis 18:10–15?
Who is fearful and what is the cause? Who created this circumstance?

Adam, Eve, Abraham, and Sarah were fearful as a consequence of the choices they made.

DAY 3
Read what God says to us in Isaiah 41:13.

➤ In Luke 2:8–9, who is fearful and what is the cause?

➤ Who is fearful and what is the cause here: Matthew 1:20? Who created this circumstance?

➤ Read Matthew 14:22–32.
Who is fearful and what is the cause? Who created this circumstance?

Even though the shepherds, Joseph, the disciples, and Peter had no control over these external forces, we can still trust in God who does have control over all things.

DAY 4
What is God saying to you in John 14:1?

➤ What are some of the causes of your fears? You answered this earlier.

➤ Does the way you were raised have an impact on or create your fears?

➤ Do you believe others might reject you, and are you afraid to show your fears? Why or why not?

➤ Read Isaiah 54:4.

➤ Read Joshua 1:6–9, 18.
What is God saying to Joshua in all these verses?

➤ What are Timothy's fears according to 2 Timothy 1:7 and 1 Timothy 4:12?

➤ Are you living in fear of anything now? If so, why?

➤ Read 2 Corinthians 10:5b.
The first step in overcoming your fear with your faith is admitting to yourself that you are fearful. There is no shame in this.
Second step is desiring to change. We must get tired of the cycle of living a defeated life in this area.

The third step is facing your fears—how?

➤ Read Philippians 4:13.
Faith, which is our action, must override our emotions.

> "So, being courageous isn't the absence of fear, but it is facing and defeating your fear with your actions motivated by your faith in Christ Jesus."
>
> —FOUNDATIONS FOR SUCCESS IN LIFE AND RELATIONSHIPS,
> a Building Lasting Relationships (BLR) seminar

Believers in Jesus Christ don't let their emotions control actions. The *blessings* of facing our fears are many: usually our fear was greater than the actual issue; disallowing negative thoughts to translate into negative actions; abandoning enslavement to fear; awareness of situations that promote fear.

MEMORY VERSE: Joshua 1:8–9; 2 Timothy 1:7

HELPING HANDS

THE CHAIN OF FEAR
➤ Were your parents, any relatives, or someone influential to you fearful of anything? If so, what impact did their fear have on you?

➤ If you are an older sibling, did your fear of anything cause your younger siblings to fear what you feared?

➤ If you are or were fearful of someone or thing, what was your fear's initial impact on you?

➤ If you are fearful of someone or thing today, how is that affecting you?

CULTIVATING OUR FAITH

Report on your experiences with last session's Deeper Roots, More Fruit activity.

GROWING TOGETHER

➣ Why do you think God told Joshua three times in Joshua chapter one to be strong and courageous?

➣ How do you define fear? Does it ever surprise you what some people are afraid of? Why? Have you surprised or disappointed yourself by what you are afraid of? Why?

➣ Do you think, if you had childhood fears, that they have a negative impact on you as an adult? Why?

Do leaders ever have fear?
➣ According to Genesis 3:6–9, what caused Adam and Eve to fear God?

➣ Strong-willed leaders like Saul, Abraham, and Sarah were fearful at times. What created their fears?

➣ Have you ever thought that your decisions and the consequences of your decisions can create fear for you?

➣ How does what God is saying in these two verses make you feel? Why?

➤ Read 2 Timothy 1:7.
A few steps that may help overcome fear through faith in Christ
  • The first step in overcoming fear with faith is admitting to oneself the fear of someone or something.
  • Desire to defeat fear.
  • Become tired of being defeated by your fear.
  • Face your fear.
  • Allow faith in Christ to motivate action and override emotion. Don't let emotions control actions.

Being courageous isn't the absence of fear, but it is facing and defeating fear with your actions motivated by your faith in Christ Jesus.

The blessings of facing your fears
- You usually discover that your fear was greater than the actual situation
- You are no longer a slave to your fear
- You cease to feel defeated by fear, affects your view of you (self-worth)
- You will be less fearful the next time you are in a possible fearful situation
- The positive effects go on and on!

BEARING FRUIT

MEMORY VERSES: Joshua 1:8–9; 2 Timothy 1:7

Before praying within your group, you'll share prayer requests. Be sure to update requests you shared in previous sessions and update the prayer notebook with how God is answering the your group's prayers. If you have a fear or a friend who has a fear, this week before the next group session, use the steps to overcoming your fear with your faith and see if they work for you.

FULFILLING

LEADER'S GUIDE

MARRIAGE RESOURCES

PRAYER JOURNAL

VIDEO LEADER'S GUIDE

https://www.clarenceshuleronline.com/discipleship-training/

Leader's Guide

Thank you for taking the challenge of leading a group! It takes courage and you'll probably learn more than your disciples.

Jesus Christ commands all of His followers to make disciples (Matthew 28:19). His first followers grew and reproduced spiritually. Jesus' challenge for Christians today is the same—to make disciples: "You have heard me teach things that have been confirmed by many reliable witnesses. Now teach these truths to other trustworthy people who will be able to pass them on to others." (2 Timothy 2:2). This workbook encourages this deeper spiritual growth through continued discipling.

Please refer to the book introduction, "The Challenge: Who, What, and How."

Discipleship makes so much sense. There's no substitute for discipleship. Mentoring is valuable, however, may not require spiritual reproduction. Biblical discipleship's group dynamics provides a "greenhouse" for cultivating spiritual growth. Not to mention the motivation that being in a safe place with a group creates.

It's often easier to learn how to reproduce in the context of small group, which helps to increase the reality of sharing what has been learned with others, plus bonding and encouragement. I imagine the disciples experienced this with Jesus and each other. Also, there is value in exposure to more than one perspective; from a peer and not only the teacher.

Few people know how to find a mentor. Disciple-makers intentionally look for and recruit future disciples, as Jesus did when He called disciples to follow Him. May God continue to richly bless you as you study and apply His Word to intentionally nurture disciples and help them to grow and reproduce.

This course is designed for a small group of 4-12 people, including the facilitator. It can also be used in a class setting (If using a class setting, consider focusing only on the Growing Together portion of the session or dividing each session into two, in order to complete sessions). Be careful and sensitive to group interaction, paying special attention to quiet participants. A large class can lower interaction. The small group generally produces better group dynamics and provides more time flexibility.

Although this course is oriented toward Christ followers, people searching for God may join your group. Through this course, Christians and non-Christians alike can find answers to spiritual questions.

➤ **Consider meeting somewhere other than a church; a house, apartment or college campus center can create a climate of community and safety. Meeting in a home** usually helps people relax more than in a church. Be open to rotating sessions to different homes or apartments, if this is of interest to the group. Providing group members the opportunity to host a meeting (if they so desire) is another way to build community.

➤ **An essential part of this course is what your disciples do between the group sessions.** Strongly encourage participants to commit to completing each session. Group sessions have been created in such a way that a person can participate and benefit from a session without having completed the "through the week" assignments. However, the discipleship experience will be enriched with the personal application components. It will also be mutually beneficial to the entire group when everyone is prepared to participate in group interactions.

➤ **Be sure to lead by example by doing the application parts yourself!** You'll be glad you did! As integral as the personal application parts of each session are, group members should be encouraged to attend every session regardless.

➤ **A key dynamic is group interaction.** To assist in getting everyone involved, the group questions and activities are designed to be interactive and relational.

You'll find suggested use of subgroups for various questions and activities. If you have a "large" group (more than 12 people), consider having subgroups of 4 to 7 people work through the Growing Together questions. Don't have the same people in the same small groups each time—avoid cliques. Be sure to keep people on topic because this helps keep the group on schedule, giving everyone a chance to participate in discussions. Having a co-leader (including an apprentice leader) can help facilitate a subgroup. Keep in mind that leadership chemistry is critical for your group.

➤ **Open-ended discussion questions create interaction among group members.** This is essential for effective and beneficial group dynamics, key to your disciples' growth. Every response deserves respect, even if it does not meet your expectations. (*Possible responses will be marked by parentheses.*)

➤ **Be spiritually prepared by praying daily, a week or more before day/ evening of the discipleship group's first session and every session.** Secure a prayer support group to pray for you and your family daily. You are now on the front lines of spiritual warfare, so don't be surprised by the possible crazy, strange, or unusual things that may happen before your first session, and after each session

LET'S GET ACQUAINTED

Welcome to your first meeting! Use these notes for this session. Expect this first session to be somewhat unstructured because you're organizing the group.

➤ **Create a "safe place" for group intimacy.** Allow everyone to get acquainted socially and spiritually as well as develop trust in you as their servant leader.

➤ **Set a friendly climate** by warmly greeting each person on arrival. Try knowing their names before this first session is over. It communicates you care; a critical step for trust in you.

➤ **Greet late-comers, realizing this may be the most critical and difficult session for people to attend.** Our enemy certainly doesn't want them there. So don't take it personally if and when people are late. If it is a couple, one spouse may have had to drag the other one—so please do not make jokes about people arriving late, even with the people who are on time. Detrimental remarks may be all that a hesitant person has to hear to use as an excuse not to join this "group of insensitive people." Welcome people without making them feel guilty for being late.

➤ **Serve inexpensive refreshments**; doing so first may be a good way to "cover" for some latecomers (if host can afford to provide refreshments— if not, then, ask group to help you cover this cost.). This also may save latecomers from missing the beginning of this session (optional).

GETTING STARTED

Briefly summarize the *Challenge* and answer questions they may have. And encourage them to keep a notebook or journal. If they have more in-depth questions, explain that participants will experience more clarity as they go through this course. Now, ask everyone to turn to **Challenge** 1. Mention the Deeper Roots, More Fruit activities at the end of each session. Now you are ready to begin.

HELPING HANDS (10-15 MINUTES)

Share *The Challenge* objective in your own words. See if there are questions. Keep to 3 minutes or less if possible. Don't chase rabbits here. If you get difficult questions—tell them you will answer later—but do make sure to answer before this session ends.

Initiate the first two or three Helping Hands question sessions by speaking about yourself first. By the second or third session, people should begin volunteering. Then you'll ask, "Who's next?" If no one responds quickly, draft someone you know fairly well. If you don't know anyone, draft the person who arrived first for this session. Don't make it a big deal. Have fun with it. But it is one of several crucial first steps in creating a safe community. Introductions can follow this pattern. Tell:

➤ One fact people may be surprised to know about you.
➤ A favorite hobby or interest you have, or would like *if* you have time.
➤ Your occupation.
➤ How long you have been a Christ follower or where you see yourself in your spiritual journey.

GROUP DIRECTORY

Collect names, phone numbers, and email addresses for a group directory.

Transition from the personal information to the spiritual by saying something like, "Now that we have each other's personal info, let's see why everyone is here." Ask the first question under Great Expectations: *How did you hear about this study?* (Church announcement.) You are looking for short, general answers with these questions. To see how people open up, possible future leaders, and how to serve the group as you lead.

GROWING TOGETHER (50 TO 60 MINUTES)

➤ How did you hear about this study?
➤ What sparked your interest about this discipleship course?

If at all possible, stay in one group. Based on your observation of who is talkative and who is not, balance as you prepare to split the group into two for this first session. Tell them tell they have 30 minutes. Suggest each group have a timekeeper and a spokesperson. Punctuality communicates respect for one another.

Apostle Paul tells about his journey to faith in Christ in Acts. Form two groups, with each group taking one of the following Scripture passages. Remember, subgroups will report findings to the larger group about Acts 22:1-22; Acts 26:1-23.

Each group will read a passage and then discuss questions 1-4. Make sure each group stops on time, then, have their group spokesperson report. After hearing from both groups, move on as quickly as you can to the Faith Story.

CULTIVATING OUR SPIRIT (15 TO 20 MINUTES)

Have one or two of your disciples share how they came to know Christ. Then share your Faith Story in 3-5 minutes—should include: what your life was like before Christ, what sparked your interest in Christ, how you actually accepted Christ into your life--include the Gospel, then briefly what your life has been like since receiving Christ into your life. Then, let group compare their Faith Story with yours to see if there is any difference. Usually, the Gospel isn't included and the emphasis is usually on their life after Christ.

Ask the entire group this question: *How are these two Acts accounts about Paul similar, yet different (22:1-22; 26:1-23)?* After each group has answered these questions, choose a spokesperson to give a report to the entire group.

Hopefully, now, you are seeing your individuals becoming a safe community. Ask if there are any questions regarding this first session. Keep answers short. If questions relate to next week, then share that you will answer that question next week.

Another step toward group intimacy and creating a safe place will be the sharing of prayer concerns. Let them know they can write down prayer requests on the Prayer Request page. Explain to them that you will close in prayer until the group does the session on prayer. This will also help those who have never prayed aloud or may be uncomfortable praying in a group, especially with people they don't know very well.

Ask for the possibility of a place to meet next week, as you desire to rotate this study in various homes. Adjourn.

BEARING FRUIT (10 TO 15 MINUTES)

Before closing this gathering in prayer, take a few minutes to share prayer requests. You will want to record these in a journal or in another careful way. Until your gathering on prayer, you as a leader will pray aloud on behalf of the group. Only some people are comfortable praying aloud, especially with people they don't know well. You don't want people to feel pressured. This is part of creating a *safe space*.

Also record anything else you want to remember.

PART 1: GETTING TO KNOW JESUS

Meeting Jesus

Remember, discipleship is *relationship*. As you prepare to facilitate this session, ask God for spiritual sensitivity regarding your participants *before* you teach them spiritual lessons. Always let them know that **they are more important than the course.** Find out how their week and day went. Demonstrate concern for them as individuals. See if they're spiritually prepared to begin the study. Ask: **"Were you able to complete the material for this session?"**

Don't be surprised if some of your disciples didn't do or complete this lesson. Try not to look shocked or disappointed. They may not have put their study time into their schedule yet and underestimated the time required to complete the material. Listen compassionately and patiently to their reasons. This may be the first time that they have ever been exposed to anything like this. Their lack of biblical knowledge may have created problems for them. They may be overwhelmed.

Encourage them to try working on their material for 20-25 minutes each day (maybe after they do their daily devotions if they have them). Gently let them know that the more they invest, the more they and others will benefit from their investment. They may not realize that they are in a spiritual war with Satan, who doesn't fight fair. So, explain to your disciples that there will be all kinds of obstacles attempting to prevent them from completing their material each week, memorizing the assigned verses, getting to the discipleship meetings, getting there on time, getting babysitters (if they need one), etc. Your disciples need to be aware and alert. It's your responsibility as a servant leader to be prepared for your disciples!

Ask those who didn't do or complete their prep work for the session, "Do you think they will be able to complete their lesson next week?" "Why or why not?" Do this without embarrassing them in front of the group, or condescending. This approach works if you have created a "Safe Place." It is usually seen as a caring act, which usually cements their commitment. Help your disciples in training to see the "big picture," that it takes discipline. Explain (don't preach or lecture) that it is a commitment to the Lord, the others in the group and those future disciples (John 17:20, 21).

Be careful not to let one person dominate your interactive discussions. If one person continues to raise his or her hand or blurts out answers, suggest, "Let's have someone who hasn't answered a question to please respond." This allows you to get more group interaction. If this doesn't work, then after the study is over, one-on-one, with no audience, ask him or her to help you: "(Name), you are so good and it is obvious you are prepared for our sessions. I've observed that some in our group may be a little insecure, so they don't speak up right away. They may feel since you have such good insight, why should they say anything. Will you help me to get them more involved by not answering immediately? You can still have input, which I need and want, this just helps others as we are creating community."

HELPING HANDS (15-20 MINUTES)

Have everyone share. This allows everyone to hear everyone's story, which accelerates developing intimacy and trust within your group. If more than 10 disciples, then in order to save time, you may then want to divide into groups of 3 or 4. Have the entire group share as quickly as possible in order to create community as quickly as possible. This results in a "Safe Place" for your interaction, which key for group dynamics. You may go over time for this meeting, but the immediate benefits from my perspective are well worth it. It is your call. If possible, everyone needs to hear everyone's story. You can lead a group of 12 including yourself, you just have to be good at time management (watching the clock) and keeping the group from feeling rushed.

Participants will provide their faith stories to you at this time. Have smaller groups reassemble into one large group again in order to answer questions for Growing Together.

GROWING TOGETHER (50 TO 60 MINUTES)

You want your disciples to know without any doubt that God loves them! This can't be overstated. This is totally different from *religion* in which humans are trying to find God and earn love. Religion is typically man seeking to please by obeying rules through self-effort. Ask one or two disciples to respond to Number 4.

Yes, God, Jesus' Father, loves us! God thought about each person before He created them (Genesis 1:26). God also gave us His DNA—we are made in His image (Genesis 1:26-27). He also gave us dominion because He wants us to experience what it feels like to reign—because He reigns! In Genesis 1:28, when it reads God blessed them—it translates: Wow! He looks at us like a father does a newborn! God praises us because we look like Him. With God being omniscient (all-knowing), He knew we humans would mess up. And He made us anyway! We should. We have His DNA!

Christianity is a personal relationship with Jesus Christ, Who empowers us to do the things He asks through the Holy Spirit, Who lives in followers of Jesus Christ (Romans 8:9-11).

CULTIVATING OUR SPIRIT (15-20 MINUTES)

Ask "Who would like to recite one of our memory verses?" You want to create an atmosphere of expectancy, with grace. Remind them that this is a challenge. Reassure them that you know it is difficult—but again let them see the "big picture" of discipleship. Ask them if they want to change the world for Christ! Ask them to reread the Introduction and A Word from the Author. For those who didn't memorize, see if you can help them devise a memory plan and a day to review their verses. Again, encourage them to come whether they have learned their verses or not. Remember, they are more important than their verses.

BEARING FRUIT_(10-15 MINUTES)

Share prayer requests (don't forget prayer request sheet). Give an opportunity for any brief testimonies about answered prayer. After prayer, agree on who will host next. Try rotating homes and apartments if possible, which allows everyone ownership of the group. Adjourn.

Cultivating Our Spiritual Passion

HELPING HANDS (15-20 MINUTES)

Continue to let them experience your love and concern, modeling what it means to disciple others. Greet everyone and ask how they're doing. Then open with a brief prayer for everyone and your time together. Keep comments brief during the introduction.

Ask **"Who has memorized their verses and wants to recite them?"** Be gentle, but a little firmer as you want them to understand the critical nature of memorizing verses for their relationship with Christ, personal lives, and those they desire to disciple in the future. Again, encourage them to come whether they have learned their verses or not. Remember, they are more important than their verses. Remind them of the memorizing verse tips in chapter one.

Return faith stories (testimonies) to your disciples with your written comments. Make sure there are positive comments, especially if you made corrections or suggestions. Gently remind disciples that they should be able to communicate their faith stories in 3 to 5 minutes. People can always ask to hear more, but we don't want to abuse the time they give us. Visit the Discipleship page on www.clarenceshuler.com for evaluating Faith Stories.

Ask if there are any questions from last week's lesson. Only take one to three. If there are complex questions, offer to meet individually if that is needed. Always keep an eye on the time as you want to be a good steward of it by not going over time. If people want to stay longer to talk with you fine, or schedule a time meet individually during the week.

Think of this session goal as preparing your disciples to spiritually survive on their own and to eventually train others. Your discipling them lays the spiritual groundwork for them discipling others!

Ask disciples what they have been previously taught about eternal security or once saved, always saved. Only take one or two if they are complex questions about eternal security, but offer to meet individually if that is requested. If the entire group has questions, then, you may delay this week's lesson for a week with permission of the group. Don't rush this. Ask who taught them their particular belief on this doctrine. This can be an emotionally charged topic so tread softly, but drive the direction of discussion as you move through the material that follows.

Their answers form a guide as to how to lead them and for which ones this may be emotionally difficult. You ask the questions and let your disciples respond. Everyone doesn't have to answer or go in a circle.

Understanding the Holy Spirit

Ask your discipleship group, "How would you explain the Trinity?" Remind them that as they study these lessons, it is for them to learn, but also think about effectively communicating these truths for when you are leading your own discipleship group.

As a former pornography addict, the most difficult first step is admitting the addiction. The second is saying no to desire, then overriding with positive actions, and not yielding to . . . the sin. Boundaries, an alternative crisis plan, an accountability partner, and most importantly, the power of the Holy Spirit finally gave me victory in this area. Also seeing that sin only gives short-term pleasure with long-term consequences! You are probably thinking that *I have issues.* You're right! I do! Only by God's grace and the Holy Spirit living in me that is making all the difference!

Consider asking one of your disciples to open this group time in a brief prayer for your disciples and your time together. Then ask your disciples how their week went. You always want to continue the personal touch.

For this Helping Hands activity you will need to make sure you have several sheets of paper and pens. Also, before doing this activity, you need to create a simple drawing of basic geometric shapes that touch or intersect.

HELPING HANDS (15-20 MINUTES)
This is critical that you answer all your questions with Bible verses supporting your answers. If there are different perspectives, then encourage their answers with Scriptural support in context—great opportunity to put last week's lesson into practice.

GROWING TOGETHER
Ask participants how they would explain to a friend who the Holy Spirit is.

For questions, go around the room asking disciples to respond to each verse or verses. You only need one answer for each verse. When you ask for volunteers for Question 5, don't press anyone to answer this question. If everyone does answer, it is a good indication that your group has become a community and this group is a "safe place." If not, just know as people are different, so are groups. Some groups jell more quickly than others.

During **"How should we live?"** share how the Holy Spirit helps you and how you yield to the Spirit. Share Romans 8:16. Explain that, the Holy Spirit lets us know that we are God's children supernaturally. For those who are Christians, help them to recall. if they heard God's Word in their mind and sensed a small voice or urging or an impression—all of these could have been the Holy Spirit communicating with them. Tell them the more time they spend reading, praying and memorizing God's Word, the clearer His voice will be to them—but it may be different for everyone in the group.

CULTIVATING OUR SPIRIT (15-20 MINUTES)
Ask participants to review the memory verses in pairs.: Galatians 2:20; Ephesians 5:17-18. Encourage everyone to keep a prayer notebook (explain).

BEARING FRUIT (10-15 MINUTES)
➤ **Share prayer requests.** By now, your disciples should be getting the "hang" of praying conversationally short 3-4 sentence prayers (at the most) per person about one thing at a time. People don't have to pray in order around the circle, nor does everyone have to pray. People can pray as often as they like about different personal issues. The idea is to pray for and about each other—not neighbors, all the missionaries in the world—unless it's a witnessing opportunity, etc.). After 30 seconds of silence, leader closes in prayer.
➤ Agree on a place to meet next week. You can call your disciples individually this week to get their opinion of this week's session and to encourage them for this upcoming week. Pray with them is they have time.
➤ Adjourn.

Praying—Talking With God

Note: In Psalm 57, David actually begins praising God *before God delivers him!*

HELPING HANDS (15-20 MINUTES)
Greet disciples and see how they have been doing. Ask if there are any

questions from last week's lesson that didn't get asked. Initiate the Helping Hands section by asking for a few to share.

GROWING TOGETHER

If you have a large group, form smaller groups to answer the group discussion questions. At the end of the Growing Together section, allow time for subgroups to report their answers to the whole group.

In question 1, *fellowship* here literally means that Jesus wants us to "Hang Out" with Him or to continually be in His face.

Explain that in the Bible it seems most people met with God in the morning. Also explain that these verses are examples and not commands. If you aren't a morning person, then, have your time alone with God another time of the day, when you are fresh, alert, and won't be interrupted. Be honest with yourself. Let your disciples know that they aren't less spiritual if they have their time alone with God other than in the morning. The most important thing is to have alone time with God.

PART 2: GROWING

Bowing to the Lord Jesus

You know the drill: ask your disciples how their week went. Continue the personal touch—letting them experience your constant love and concern.

➤ **Consider opening this group time in a brief prayer for your disciples and your time together.** Be sure to "Thank" God for the gift of the indwelling Holy Spirit, Who is always with all followers of Christ.

➤ **Ask everyone how did they like praying conversationally?** Short 3-4 sentence prayers (at the most) per person about one thing at a time. People don't have to pray in order around the circle, nor does everyone have to pray. People can pray as often as they like about different personal issues (idea is to pray for and about each other, not neighbors, all the missionaries in the world, unless witnessing opportunity). After 30 seconds of silence, leader closes in prayer.

➤ **Explain the Prayer Request page and the Prayer Notebook.** Encourage your disciples to keep a **prayer notebook** that might include Scriptures, insights, Words from the Holy Spirt, prayer needs, prayers for others, and desires of their hearts. You may point them to the Psalms for examples of what David prayed. Also encourage them to create a **Prayer Request** page similar to the one on page 71 so that they can track their prayers and how they were answered. Your disciples may choose to use the Prayer Journal in the back of this book.

HELPING HANDS (15-20 MINUTES)

➤ **Watch for those individuals who may appear to be uncomfortable.** For this session, you may need to give your thoughts on why God is your ultimate boss, if your disciples seem hesitant.

➤ **Discussing the term "Lordship," may be a foreign concept to your disciples**, especially if they were born in America, which has never had a King or Queen. The closest public figure America has to royalty is a president. No matter your political preference, the president doesn't have absolute authority. This is totally opposite from understanding Jesus Christ as Lord. Don't allow a political discussion because politics can divide your community.

GROWING TOGETHER (50 TO 60 MINUTES)

➤ **Jesus Christ has earned the right to be Lord** because He is the Creator of humans, earth and the physical heavens. We exist only because God wanted us. He was beaten beyond recognition for our sakes—dying one of the most brutal deaths known to man, even though He was innocent! He gives us eternal life and a godly destiny! He is exactly the kind of Lord I want! What about you?

➤ **Have your disciples recite Luke 9:23-25.** Ask them what it means to them. There are at least 4 actions that are required to experience Christ's Lordship: (1) we must stop our selfish ways; (2) daily take up our cross, which includes all of our responsibilities and privileges as Christ followers; (3) follow Him – its not about feeling, but obedience; and (4) be willing to die for Christ's purposes.

    Mark 1:17 includes our daily taking up our cross. It is telling people who don't know Jesus Christ about Him. Whether they accept or reject Him is between God and them. **The results are His, our job is just to tell them.** We can tell them by using our Faith Story. Encourage your disciples to pray for opportunities—for God to give you favor with the person with whom you wish to share. If it is a co-worker, only share before work, during breaks or at lunch. Don't talk about Jesus when you should be working. That would be a bad reflection on Jesus Christ. Often, but not always, the key in seeing people accept Christ is obedience.

Ask your disciples to quote Luke 6:46. This is a perfect place for it!

CULTIVATING OUR SPIRIT (15 TO 20 MINUTES)

Here is another opportunity for you to evaluate if your disciples have become a community. This is a place for vulnerability. Vulnerability happens when there is trust.

➤ **Share what has, can or is hindering you from consistently experiencing Christ's Lordship.** Your sharing makes it easier for someone else to share. It also models spiritual leadership. **Christ never asks us to do something He didn't do first!**

➤ **Legalism occurs when we are more concerned with rules than people.** Don't break rules unless you are willing to pay the consequences!

➤ **Soon after Gary Chapman introduced me to a personal relationship with Jesus Christ,** I memorized the entire New Testament book of James. I memorized the book, not to glorify God, but to impress Gary. Memorizing God's Word was great, but I did it for the wrong reason! I wanted a man's affirmation. My biological father loved me, but didn't know how to communicate his love because his father never did to for him.

➤ **No pressure here.** Ask with expectation. If you think someone doesn't have a personal relationship with Jesus, hopefully, you've been praying daily or at least weekly for their salvation.

➤ **If someone did accept Christ, you should display excitement, even if you are normally unemotional. Let this person or persons know you're happy for them!**

BEARING FRUIT (10 TO 15 MINUTES)

➤ **See if anyone is struggling with the concept of Jesus as their Lord.** Be sensitive as you close in prayer to what you have heard prayed before you pray. Without embarrassing anyone, let your prayer be one of assurance and encouragement. Short 3-4 sentence prayers (at the most) per person about one thing at a time. **People don't have to pray in order around the circle, nor does everyone have to pray.** People can pray as often as they like about different personal issues (the idea is to pray for and about each other, not neighbors, all the missionaries in the world, unless witnessing opportunity, etc.). After 30 seconds of silence, leader closes in prayer. Encourage everyone to keep a **prayer notebook.**

➤ **Agree on a place to meet next week.** Call your disciples individually this week to get their opinion of this week's session and encourage them for this upcoming week. Pray with them if they have time. Adjourn

Wearing God Glasses

➤ **Ask one of your disciples (if they have already prayed aloud) to open this group time in a brief prayer for your disciples and your time together.** Don't ask someone who has never prayed in front of the group because this might embarrass him/her. Then ask your disciples how their week went. You always want to continue the personal touch—letting them experience your constant love and concern.

➤ **As the group leader, make sure you are prayed up and have people praying for your** disciples and you because the enemy would love to cause a problem during this session. Be sensitive to people and read body language if you know how to and are good at it.

➤ **Ask the Holy Spirit for His wisdom as you lead this session.** Ask for Him to protect all of you from the evil one and for the Holy Spirit to have free reign in the session tonight and that God the Father will be glorified!

HELPING HANDS (15-20 MINUTES)

➤ **Be careful here.** Talking about politics can be volatile. Bring up the point of how Christians in one political party can prejudge Christians who belong to another political party or how Christians who belong to different denominations can do the same. **Avoid terms such as "Liberal" and "Conservative."** You want to focus on individuals, not groups. Don't lose track of time or control of the group. **This is your call whether or not you use this suggestion.**

➤ **Don't allow any type of rejection** if a person shares something negative he or she did. Thank him or her for having the courage to share. Sharing is a sign of community.

202

GROWING TOGETHER (50 TO 60 MINUTES)

➤ **Step 1.** Jesus breaks a Jewish traditional law by traveling into Samaria (may need to explain who the Samaritans were)

➤ **Step 2.** Jesus went to Samaria where she lived (the Great Commission).

➤ **Step 3.** Jesus meets her on her own turf, the well, where there were other women in her town.

➤ **Step 4.** Jesus breaks another traditional law by speaking to a Samaritan woman who was always seen by a Jew as ceremonially unclean, which means He defiled Himself by speaking with her.

➤ **Step 5.** Jesus makes Himself vulnerable to the woman by asking for help (water).

➤ **Step 6.** Jesus demonstrates staying power when the woman initially rejects Him. He doesn't go away.

Jesus was focusing on the woman's needs, not His own. He was focusing on giving, not receiving. These six steps are excerpts from my book, *Winning the Race to Unity: Is Racial Reconciliation Really Working?*

➤ **Remind your disciples that biblical love is an action.** Ask someone to quote Luke 9:23-25. And ask someone else to quote Luke 6:46. This helps your disciples to realize memorizing is not just for the group session, but for living the Christian life like Christ.

CULTIVATING OUR SPIRIT (15 TO 20 MINUTES)

In light of the Bible verses in this session, ask your group to comment on James Baldwin's quote:

> "I think you owe it to me, as my friend, to fight me, to let me get away with nothing, to force me to be clear, to force me to be honest, to allow me to take no refuge in rage or in despair…and of course, I owe you the same. This means we are certainly going to hurt each other's feelings from time to time. But that's one of the ways in which people learn from each other."

BEARING FRUIT (10 TO 15 MINUTES)

➤ **After listening to all the comments, bring some closure.** More closure will come after the session on **Forgiveness**.

➤ Remind your disciples about the Big Picture of God's Love and Forgiveness. Tell disciples that you will respond more in the Forgiveness Session.

➤ Forgiving a person who hurt you doesn't mean you'll become or that you should be best friends (that's not the goal); but forgiveness is the first step toward your emotional healing (freedom) from a past hurtful situation. Neither does forgiving mean you'll ever forget it, but the event's emotional grip on you is no longer as strong as it once was. *Don't let the pain of your past punish your present, paralyze your future. and pervert your purpose because You have a godly destiny!*

➤ Be sensitive to any disciples who may be frustrated or confused with this session. Encourage conversational prayer. You close as always. If necessary pray for all of your disciples by name, being sensitive to their feelings on this issue. Individually, call any distressed disciples this week—the sooner the better. Be available after this session to talk or make appointments for next week before the group time. After 30 seconds of silence, leader closes in prayer. Encourage everyone to keep a **prayer notebook**. Secure a place to meet next week. Adjourn.

Forgiving and Healthier Living

Ask one of your disciples (if they have previously prayed aloud at a session's closing) to open group time in a brief prayer for your disciples and your time together. **You're beginning to transition your disciples from students to leaders—disciple makers.** Don't ask someone who hasn't prayed in front of the group. This might embarrass him/her. You know the routine of asking your disciples how their week was. They need to experience your constant love and concern.

➤ Make sure you prayed. Have people praying for your disciples and you. Our enemy wants to cause a problem during this session. Be sensitive to people and read body language if you know how and are good at it.

➤ Ask the Holy Spirit for His wisdom and protection from the evil one as you lead this session. Ask for the Holy Spirit to have free reign during the session and for God's will.

➤ Be aware and sensitive because some or most of your disciples may have people whom they trusted who abused them in some manner. So even the thought of forgiveness may be extremely difficult for them.

➤ This session may take longer to complete, so watch your time. Try finishing on time, but don't make your disciples feel rushed. Your disciples are always more important than finishing on time. Get their permission to go over scheduled time. **Must be unanimous.**

HELPING HANDS (15-20 MINUTES)

➤ Ask disciples what is a sincere apology?

- **Don't rush.** Your disciples' responses may be a preview for your session.
- **Listen carefully as your disciples share.** Hopefully, by now community has been established and is full blown! People are now sharing with no hesitation because there is no fear of judgment or rejection. Sharing here should produce more intimacy.

GROWING TOGETHER (50 TO 60 MINUTES)

➤ **Before engaging in this section, give your disciples the option not to answer.** But take mental notes of how your disciples are responding because some may need emotional and spiritual healing from the pain of their past. They may need some one-on-one time with you or a biblical counselor you trust. **Watch the time.** You want to finish on time, but your disciples' spiritual condition is more critical than time. You may need to spend another evening to complete this session. If so, discuss it with your disciples, but only if you know you won't finish in the scheduled time.

➤ **Get three disciples to answer** the question regarding the difficulty of forgiving someone. Ask one for a definition of forgiveness before using a dictionary; one for the dictionary's definition of forgiveness; and one for God's definition of forgiveness.

➤ **Remind disciples that forgiveness isn't an emotion.** Tell them believers are commanded to forgive; but there is a difference between biblical forgiveness and emotional healing. **There is no timetable on emotional healing.**

➤ **Biblical love according to Christ's example in Mark 14:32-36, is an action**, not an emotion. So biblically, followers of Christ can't fall out of love. And we can love people we don't like with actions towards them, which glorify God.

➤ **Ask your disciples to quote Luke 17:4.** Help them see that the same person sinned against another person seven different times in one day!

205

WOW! Each time the person who sinned repented and asked the person that was sinned against for forgiveness for that particular sin (7 different sins against the same person), the offended believer is commanded to forgive. Repent means to stop doing the sin. **Biblical forgiveness, then, has nothing to do with our emotions. There is a difference between biblical forgiveness and emotional healing.**

Because I tend to hold grudges regarding forgiveness, God has me pray Blessings for my enemies. It is difficult to stay angry with someone for whom you are consistently praying.

    Repeat, **"There is a difference between forgiveness and your emotional healing!"** Emotional healing takes time and varies with different people. But it isn't an excuse to remain in pain or have a prolonged self-pity party.

CULTIVATING OUR SPIRIT (15 TO 20 MINUTES)
Be ready to explain what God means when He says He won't forgive us if we don't forgive (Matthew 6:14-15). It isn't that God doesn't want to forgive us, but our refusing to forgive someone, makes us incapable of accepting God's forgiveness because of the hardness of our hearts at that time. Our heart is like a closed fist-nothing can get in or out of it. It has nothing to do with our salvation. It is all about our fellowship with God, not our relationship with Him.
➤ **Be ready to explain repentance**
➤ **Some of your disciples may struggle forgiving themselves.** Some people feel unworthy of it; some people don't understand it, or God's perspective on forgiveness. They haven't experienced forgiveness themselves, so they have difficulty forgiving others.

BEARING FRUIT (10 TO 15 MINUTES)
➤ **My quote may be helpful,** *"Don't let the pain of your past punish your present, paralyze your future, and pervert your purpose because you have a godly destiny."* There's no guarantee that the suggestions in this section will work for everyone.
➤ **What does emotionally letting go of the hurt look or feel like for you?** It is not rehearsing the hurt, which stirs up all the pain involved with the wound. It's like pulling the scab off of a wound before it is healed. A scab

usually falls off a healed wound. You treat it with medication while it is healing, but seldom focus all your energy on it. It isn't a denial of your pain, but it is moving forward to your healing
➤ **Be sensitive to disciples who may be frustrated or confused with this session.**

Use the same closing procedure: briefly sharing answers to prayer, conversational prayer, you closing in prayer after 30 seconds of silence. If necessary, pray for those who shared their struggle with forgiveness. Thank them for their courage to share and their trusting the group. Be available at session's conclusion and call distressed disciples individually before the next group time (sooner is better).

Growing Deeper Roots

➤ **Do weekly check-in:** Have a disciple open with brief prayer and ask how the disciples week is going.
➤ **Ask if there are any unanswered questions from last week's session.** Only take one or two if they are complex questions regarding forgiveness. Offer to meet individually if requested. If the entire group has questions, you may delay this week's lesson for a week with group's permission. Try not to if possible, but be sensitive to the group's need.

HELPING HANDS (15-20 MINUTES)
➤ **Your goal for this section is to help disciples in applying the truths of the Bible to their lives.** This is a critical section because you need to see if your disciples can feed themselves. **If they can feed themselves from God's Word then, they will soon be able to teach others to feed themselves.** Don't expect or demand that all your disciples will arrive at this point simultaneously.

GROWING TOGETHER (50 TO 60 MINUTES)
➤ **If you do divide into subgroups, it is critical for the entire group to hear all answers. This helps them evaluate if they can feed themselves from the Bible.**

➤ **Be clear here that you are not talking about daily reading the Bible,** but taking time to study it in detail.

➤ **Be careful here to guard your time** and in the next section, Bible Study Tools, everyone doesn't need to answer. Two or three answers are fine.

➤ **Drop anchor when you get to the Bible Study Tools.** Hear how your disciples used their surgical tools to operate. What truths were they able to discover and how did they apply these truths to their personal lives? Share your truths and personal applications, but you go last.

➤ **Now, you are in the meat of this session,** you want to hear from everyone. So if you go over time, it is okay; but get the group's permission or to continue this next week. **But this is a key session**—to evaluate your communicating effectiveness, disciples' commitment, discovering potential disciple-makers in your group.

CULTIVATING OUR SPIRIT (15 TO 20 MINUTES)
➤ **Quote memory verses:** John 15:7; Philippians 4:6-7

BEARING FRUIT (10 TO 15 MINUTES)
➤ **You know the session closing procedure:** sharing of answered prayer and conversational group prayer, agreeing on place for next week's session, and adjourn.

PART 3: DISCOVERING

Following Forever

Continue opening procedure. Keep comments brief. This session will go quickly-watch the time.

➤ **Hopefully, your disciples feel secure enough with each other and you to freely express themselves without fear of condemnation.**

➤ **Your disciples need to understand and embrace, that to those who accept Jesus Christ as their Savior, He gives them eternal life.** If they can lose their salvation, it may be a good one, **but certainly not an eternal one!**

➤ **Don't be condescending to anyone in the group.** Don't drop anchor here-keep pressing forward. Communicate this truth if appropriate, here-almost in passing.

➤ **Know that not every Christ follower believes this.** This issue is not one that Christians should fight about. Encourage them to use their Bible Study methods and tools to reexamine this teaching and to come to their own conclusion.

➤ **Ask disciples what they have been taught about eternal security or once saved, always saved.** Only take one or two questions if they are complex about eternal security. Offer to meet individually if that is requested. If the entire group has questions, delay this week's lesson for a week with the group's permission. Don't rush this discussion. Ask who taught them their particular belief on this doctrine. This can be an emotionally charged topic. Tread softly, but drive the direction of discussion.

➤ **Their answers form a guide as to how to lead them** in this session.

HELPING HANDS (15-20 MINUTES)

Ephesians 1:13-14, is a fulfillment of John 14:15-16, in which is Jesus Christ's promise of the Holy Spirit to those who accepted Him as Savior.

➤ **Butterflies can never go back to being a caterpillar.** Chicks who crack their eggshell can never go back inside that eggshell and make it whole again. Have fun, but cut the usual time to 10 minutes or less because you'll need it for the Growing Together section.

➤ **No one can snatch Christ followers from our Heavenly Father**, not Satan or even the disciples themselves, according to Romans 8:31-39; this includes anyone created!

GROWING TOGETHER (50 TO 60 MINUTES)

➤ **If everyone doesn't join this discussion:** ((1) they may disagree with this teaching and that's okay; (2) they may believe, but it's new to them; (3) a beloved family member may reject this teaching—your disciple may feel he or she is betraying this person; or (4) there could be other reasons. **So, it is critical not to condemn.** If it gets tense, just say, 'Clarence believes. this' Make me the bad guy, so the group continues to trust you!

➤ **God's primary characteristic is His love!** These verses teach God's love is forever (Psalm 118:1-4, 29); God's love is unconditional (Hosea 3:1-4; 11:8-9); God's love requires discipline (Hebrews 12:5-11); and God initiates sharing His love with us (1 John 4:19).

➤ **Drive home the point that God, our Heavenly, Father loves us!** This session is an extremely intimate one, be sensitive, not only to answers, but to body language.
➤ **Try to discover the following:**
  • What does being "sealed" by the Holy Spirit mean to them?
  • How does that impact their understanding of sin and its affect on the Holy Spirit.
➤ **This is your example of what it means to be sealed**, kept in tack safe until heaven.

Refer to William Barclay quote in the Part 3, Day 2 section.

> **"Works" are the good acts we do because of our love for God.** *Works do not earn us salvation (Ephesians 2:8-9).* **There is no condemnation after we become Christ followers for our disobedience to God ever again because Jesus Christ's sinless life, death, burial and resurrection paid the penalty for our disobedience (sins) once and for all.** *Jesus Christ's actions simultaneously broke the law of sin and death for His followers, so death is never ever required again because of the completeness of Christ's work on the cross and His resurrection—defeating death!*

CULTIVATING OUR SPIRIT (15 TO 20 MINUTES)
➤ **Have those who would like to recite Ephesians 1:13-14.** Ask what is this verse saying. Then have them quote Ephesians 4:30

BEARING FRUIT (10 TO 15 MINUTES)
➤ Before closing this session **ask:**
  • Who primarily would want us to doubt our salvation and security?
  • How would being able to lose your salvation affect your walk with God? Would you constantly be worried about losing it?
  • Could you fall into Satan's trap of pride, thinking you can earn your salvation by your works (1 Corinthians 3:10-15)? Cults often have a works/salvation theology.
  • What do you think a "You can earn your salvation by your work" belief does to Christ's death on the cross and His resurrection? How would

such thinking influence our faith? (It diminishes it and His work is insufficient, so we have to help Him out with our works. If this is the case, do we really need Christ at all?)

➤ **The only person who wants to separate Christ followers from God is Satan.** Some of your disciples may ask you what if they change their mind and stop following Christ. In Romans 8:31-39, the passage says that **no one created, which includes Satan and us can separate us from God!**

➤ **If a Christ follower doesn't believe in eternal security,** a person might become legalistic, not experiencing all of God's grace, nor being gracious. Make sure they understand the **"timeless"** concept of the cross's power. Don't preach. Ask questions. Discuss how losing your salvation is inconsistent with God's character and what's in the Bible. These are the issues of faith and grace.

➤ **Another problem with believing a Christian can lose salvation is that believers may develop an unhealthy view of themselves in regards to salvation,** placing emphasis on themselves and not God! Such thinking may cause an individual to believe he or she had more to do with their salvation than God. This would also result in believing Christ's work is not complete.

➤ **Remind disciples that no matter what their beliefs on this topic,** that it is not a reason for Christians to fight each other. We are brothers and sisters in Christ.

➤ **Proceed with normal closing.**

Suffering and Success

Have someone you respect spiritually pray with you before meeting with your disciples. Pray for God's wisdom and protection from Satan before, during, and after this session.

➤ **Some disciples may wonder, "How can a holy God allow one of His own to suffer?"** You may get other such questions. God, our Father has all the answers. Don't be afraid to say, "I don't know, let me get back with you next week. I do trust in God's faithfulness." God will give you the words to say. This could be one of the best sessions for your disciples and you!

➤ Your community should be established to the point where disciples are sharing with no hesitation.

➤ **Your disciples should learn that God might initiate our suffering** not because of our lack of faith, but **because of our faith.** God wants to show us off to Satan. He also wants other Christ followers and those who don't know Him to see us demonstrate how we can be victorious in suffering.

➤ **God often uses suffering as a vehicle for spiritual promotion and developing intimacy with Him.** Often God allows us to suffer so that it becomes more difficult for us to sin.

➤ Sometimes our suffering is a result of our disobedience.

HELPING HANDS (15-20 MINUTES)

➤ **God often uses suffering as a vehicle for spiritual promotion and developing intimacy with Him.** Often God allows us to suffer so that it becomes more difficult for us to sin.

➤ **Sometimes our suffering is a result of our disobedience.** Some people accept Christ as their personal Savior because of these divinely appointed circumstances.

GROWING TOGETHER (50 TO 60 MINUTES)

Your disciples should know God thought about them before He created them! God, the Father discussed it with the Trinity ("Let us..."). Being omniscience (all-knowing), God knew we would sin and He still created us anyway! WOW! That to me is love! All humans, believers or not have God's DNA!

➤ **God created you, loves you, wants you, has not rejected you, and has a wonderful plan for your life!** God is not against you! He is for you!

➤ **God calls us marvelous in Psalm 139:14** (NLT), The God of all creation calls us marvelous! In verse 16, He made the days for us, not us for the days!

➤ **God calls us saints, not sinners.** Technically and biblically, Christ followers aren't sinners, but are saints who can sin. You need to know who you are!

➤ **Consider Adam and Eve being incomplete spiritually at the time of the Fall.** God is a God of development-process (for example, Creation). Adam & Eve's spiritual development is interrupted by their sin and its consequences. God's process of spiritual development continues after the Fall; but requires a different method because of our sinful nature that now naturally rebels against God. Suffering could be one of God's mechanisms for completing our spiritual development (James 1:2-4, 12). Read Isaiah 53:10-12; 1 Peter 3:18

➤ **Christians may experience suffering because:**
- One result of the Fall (Adam & Eve's sin)—consequences of sin (Psalm 90); our suffering (including deaths of loved ones) may not be the result of a specific sin, thus, making us feel our suffering is unfair or unjust. God gives us the privilege of choice. People can make bad choices.
- Reaping the consequences of our specific actions (Galatians 6:7-8)
- To test the genuineness of our faith. God knows the level of our faith, but we don't until it is tested (1 Peter 1:3-9, v.3-5 what God has done for us; v.6-9 purpose of our testing).
- Sometimes, **I believe God wants to show us off to Satan,** "Look at these followers who will not forsake Me no matter what happens to them." **Thus, we may suffer, not because of the lack of our faith, but sometimes because of our faith** (Job 1:8-12, here God initiates Job's suffering. God is using Job's faith to show him off to Satan.
- **Notice Satan has to get permission as to what he can to do saints.** Read Job 2:3-6. Look at Job's response (Job 2:7-10)
- To develop more intimacy with Christ (Philippians 3:10—the word "know" here is the same used for sexual intercourse).

➤ Jeremiah and Habakkuk weren't the only ones in the Bible to complain. What is critical is that **they weren't complaining about God to someone else. They were speaking directly to God.** They were angry and frustrated, but they didn't curse God. They came close to crossing the line, yet, didn't. They were talking to the God who could in His timing answer all their questions.

CULTIVATING OUR SPIRIT (15 TO 20 MINUTES)

Have disciples quote Job 2:10 & James 1:2-4. **When God wants to promote us spiritually, He often uses suffering to prepare us:**

➤ **To receive and appreciate His Blessings to us** (2 Corinthians 4:15-18). In this passage, there is a phrase, "light and momentary affliction/suffering." God sees all of our suffering as momentary because He sees it in the context of eternity. The next time you suffer, ask God this question, "Father, what are you trying to teach me?"

➤ **Refer back to Job who received a double portion of everything he lost except his children.** Why *didn't* he receive back a double portion of children? The twofold explanation can be found in Isaiah 7:15. First, if Job had babies or young children who were unable to distinguish good from evil, they were already in heaven. Second, Job's other children had likely reached the age at which they were able to choose right from wrong, good from evil. This implies that children have to reach what is called "the age of accountability." This is *not a specific age* but is achieved when a child *knows the difference* between good and evil.

➤ **For spiritual maturity** (James 1:2-4,12). For any temptation or suffering, God has already prepared us for it (1 Corinthians 10:13 & James 1:13-15); Psalm 66:10, "You have tested us, O God; you have purified us like silver."

BEARING FRUIT (10 TO 15 MINUTES)

When we experience suffering that isn't a result of sin, we should get excited because God is about to do something amazing in our lives, which will impact us, and those around us (believers & non-believers)!

Even when we suffer due to a direct consequence of our sin, God still provides and showers grace on us, even in His discipline of us. Usual closing

Keeping Time

➤ **Usual opening.**

➤ **Ask**, "When you filled out your first time schedule, were there any surprises about your schedule?"

➤ This is a short, but critical session because our time management is so crucial for our personal time with God, our families, fun, work, rest, and time for ourselves. Your disciples managing their time well will be important if they are to implement the biblical principles to which they are being exposed.

HELPING HANDS (15-20 MINUTES)

➤ **Get a mason jar, 6 to 7 golf balls, and uncooked beans.** Fill the jar with beans first. The beans represent all the activities we have to do during the day, prepare for work, work, household chores-washing clothes, preparing meals, community participation. Then, put the golf balls in the jar. The golf balls represent our biblical priorities, Quiet Time with God, time with spouse or significant other, or self, family time if you have one, church, making a disciple, and the like. If you put the mundane things in first, which are important, but not priorities, there isn't enough room for all the golf balls—God's priorities for you. But if you put God's priorities for you in first, there is plenty of room for all the golf balls and the beans, plus room at the top of the jar with space. So 24 hours a day is plenty! It is all about how you use your time! You will have to figure the amount of beans and number of golf balls.

➤ **Bishop Courtney McBath calls it managing time** instead of balancing, "if you are balancing, then, you are giving your family and work equal weight. When managing, you may spend more time at work, but it is only a means to an end, to better serve your family. Therefore, I work hard to create memories with my family. Sometimes, I sacrifice work, resulting in less money because I have to give more weight and time with my family. It is a choice of investment."

GROWING TOGETHER (50 TO 60 MINUTES)

Have your disciples view time as an asset, not an enemy. Their mindset needs to be managing their time, not being managed by time because time will manage you if you don't take the initiative.

➤ **Ask your disciples what are their goals.** Ask them how their goals are shaping their priorities. Ask them how do they evaluate if their priorities are helping them reach their goals-why or why not? This will provide more insight for you to help you better serve your disciples and be sensitive to them as individuals on different journeys.

➤ **Though they aren't discipling anyone yet,** ask them if can they think of people they know that this course would help or who would enjoy taking this discipleship course?

➤ **God's priorities in John 17:18-26 are:** be holy; learn God's Word/Truth; go into the world to tell others about Jesus Christ: that He came to earth to tell us about His Father, which resulted in others becoming Christ's disciples; and for spiritual unity with the Father and other disciples.

➤ **Listen to your disciples.** They may teach you a thing or two. You should be learning from your disciples. In fact, you should learn more from them, than they do from you. You don't to have answers per se; but be a cheerleader encouraging them in their creativity as they learn how to live their Christ-like life before others. Be sure to remind them to have fun in life. The Christian life isn't about being serious every moment or preaching to everyone you see. It is about managing the time God gives you. And it is not about perfection, it is about consistency.

CULTIVATING OUR SPIRIT (15 TO 20 MINUTES)
➤ **Have disciples quote memory verses:** Ephesians 5:15–16; Colossian 4:5–6. How can you make the most of your time?
➤ **After asking this question, you answer this one first.** If you want people to open up to you, you must open up to them first. Hopefully, by now, your disciples have community and safety with each other. But every group will be different and in different places. So don't assume or be disappointed with your group's intimacy or lack of it. Give them grace.

BEARING FRUIT (10 TO 15 MINUTES)
➤ **Was anyone's second time sheet different from his or her first time sheet?** If so, ask them to share why.
➤ **Field any questions your disciples may have.** Be willing to meet with any individually during the upcoming week. Usual closing. Agree on a place to meet next week and adjourn.

Discovering Destiny

➤ **Do usual opening.**
This session is for disciples to realize their potential for God and themselves! With Christ—their dreams can come true! This session is for them to gain affirmation and security in who the are in Jesus Christ as well as discovering and fulfilling God's unique purpose for them on earth.

Your disciples need to comprehend that they were created by God because He wanted them and loved them. He also has a godly destiny for them. They need to know His plan for them, which is His best for them
➤ **Ask disciples to answer the question: "Why am I here or what is my purpose?"**
➤ Ask them, **"When you ask small children what did you want to be,** how many occupations do they typically mention?" Usually, children name two or three occupations.

Use a puzzle. Drop the puzzle pieces on the floor. Give them the cover with the picture of what the puzzle is to look like. **The teaching point is** that God has the big picture. But the disciples have to put the pieces together in order to make the cover picture a reality. We have to take steps (puzzle pieces) to experience God's destiny for us.

HELPING HANDS (15-20 MINUTES)

➤ God call us marvelous (NLT) or wonderful (NIV) in Psalm 139:14! Why does He call His followers this?

According to Jeremiah 29:11 and Psalm 139:16, the application is that God has a plan for our best, not the worse!

➤ The first step to become a Christ follower is that a person must ask Jesus Christ to forgive his/her sins and come into his/her life as Savior and Lord. A second step to find your destiny after salvation is discovering your spiritual gift(s) that happens as we serve others. Typically, other Christ followers will tell you what your gift is because you are using it to serve them.

➤ As we tell people about Jesus Christ, using our spiritual gift(s)—the nature of spiritual gifts isn't for us, but to serve others with our gift, and make disciples, then, similar to a flashlight, God reveals more of His specific purpose for us. But if we're not following Christ like we should, there is no need for God to give us more direction, which we aren't going to follow.

GROWING TOGETHER (50 TO 60 MINUTES)

➤ Ask one of your disciples to read 1 John 4:18. It isn't uncommon for fearful people to feel they are unworthy of anything.

> *"Fear is the enemy of faith in Jesus Christ.*
> *Fear keeps our eyes off Jesus, the God of the impossible and keeps them focused on us-only what we can't do on our own and our present situation."*

Peace and self-control—allowing fear to dominate you is your choice. Ask one of your disciples if he or she can recite Philippians 4:13.

➤ "When I'm emotionally out of balance, I tend to look beyond myself and God for help and/or satisfaction. I feel that I'm not enough. In 1983 as a single man desperate for a relationship, fame and fulfillment, I self-seduced myself into pornography, but it created more damage, wounds and pain. God graciously delivered me from my 11-year addiction and has kept me clean since 1994. I find purpose and joy helping others defeat pornography in their lives.

➤ **Now, my peace and contentment comes from who I am in Christ.** *"God's grace is that I see His love for me through my family, other Christ followers and friends who may not know Christ. Being able to use my spiritual gifts and see their results in the transformation of others to a more fulfilling life. God has graciously let me go along for this ride! Receiving God's love through His people and learning to focus on staying in my lane—seeing what God has for me and not being jealous of someone else's success."*

CULTIVATING OUR SPIRIT (15 TO 20 MINUTES)
➤ Have disciples quote memory verses: Psalm 139:16 & Ephesians 2:10

BEARING FRUIT (10 TO 15 MINUTES)
➤ Field any questions your disciples may have. Be willing to meet with any individually during the upcoming week. Agree on a place to meet next week and adjourn.

PART 4: RELATING

Being Single and Content

➤ **Usual opening.**
➤ **Pray for sensitivity because this session for singles could touch a sensitive area for some of your disciples.** Your singles may have never been married or divorced with no children, or divorced with children, or never married with children.

Your single disciples might be children of divorce. **It is imperative they don't feel like second-class citizens as you interact on this topic of being single.** All people are created in God's image. Therefore, everyone has value and purpose regardless of their relationship status.

➤ **Some of your disciples may equate their self-worth to their relationship status.** Married couples in your group may be experiencing marital problems.

➤ This session has to be a safe place for them and possibly a healing place for all of your disciples.

HELPING HANDS (15-20 MINUTES)

➤ Emphasize that singles aren't "less than" due to their relationship status and that they shouldn't see themselves that way.

➤ If you are a Christian and single, you are *complete* before God. You don't have to date or be married to be complete before God. Don't feel that you are abnormal because you aren't in a relationship or aren't married. Don't feel pressured because well-intended family members, friends or church members keep asking you why you aren't married? It is not the intention of most to be insensitive. *Don't rush into a relationship!*

GROWING TOGETHER (50 TO 60 MINUTES)

➤ In 1 Corinthians 7, when Paul urges people to remain single it is because the "present crisis or distress" refers to persecution of Christians without any protection of the government. So Paul tells singles that it may be easier to enduring this difficult time without the additional concerns for a spouse and/or children. This "present crisis or distress" could also just be the pressures of everyday life.

Paul urging Christians to remain single could also be because of his former marriage and his wife leaving after he became a Christian. Also he feels that marriage will take away time from being totally committed to Christ (1 Corinthians 7:32-35).

➤ Joseph is approximately 17 years old when God began speaking to him through dreams. Becoming second in command of all of Egypt is Joseph's reward from God for not allowing himself to be seduced by Potiphar's wife years earlier. Not having sex with her resulted in years in prison for Joseph

➤ Sex was created by God. Sex outside of marriage usually results in destruction. Numerous secular research sources reveals that those having sex before marriage have a higher divorce rate. When they do marry after having premarital sex, they tend to have less sex. They are at a higher risk for affairs. Their children often repeat their parents' pattern in having sex before marriage. They tend to have less marital satisfaction.

CULTIVATING OUR SPIRIT (15 TO 20 MINUTES)

➤ Have disciples quote memory verses: Philippians 4:12; Proverbs 3:5–6

> "When as a single, I embraced that God loved me and that being single was His very Best for me at that time, I experienced peace. I ceased trying to *make things happen*. It really takes the pressure off. When family, dating, or married couples would make negative comments toward me about being single, I knew they meant well. They probably didn't realize how their comments sounded to a single person. I also knew God was not punishing me, nor did I need to be more spiritual.
>
> To reduce my times of being lonely I would go spend time with senior citizens or people who couldn't reimburse me in any way I thought. But these senior citizens affirmed me. They imparted so much earthly and godly wisdom. WOW! Being lonely can sometimes be a choice! Focus on giving and you'll receive so much more than you gave!"
>
> —EXCERPT FROM *Single and Free to Be Me,* p. 84

> With Christ, I can be lonely, but never alone"
>
> —PASTOR AL Pittman

BEARING FRUIT (10 TO 15 MINUTES)

Field any questions your disciples may have. Have Conversational Prayer. Be willing to meet with any individually during the upcoming week. Agree on a place to meet next week and adjourn.

Dating Mr. or Mrs. Right

➤ **Usual opening.**

Tell disciples that there will be some overlap between this session and last week's. Repeat the phrase from last week, "if you are in Christ, **you are complete**, you don't have to be in a relationship!" There may be some singles that either don't want to be in a relationship or do want to be in a relationship, but aren't having any success. Both types of singles are often made to feel abnormal by the church and other Christ followers. Make sure they are safe with you and the other disciples.

➤ **Some disciples may be wounded, even those dating or married.** Be sensitive, especially with your humor. I'm not saying not to joke, but be careful what, how, and when you say things.

➤ **It is critical that no one leaves this session feeling unloved by God** or that they are being punished by God because they aren't in a relationship

HELPING HANDS (15-20 MINUTES)

➤ **Game:** make strips of paper for everyone in your group. Mark the strips with the number one or two, depending on the number of disciples in your group. You want to have at least three people as single and the rest in pairs. Have people pick a folded strip out of a bowl. After everyone has selected a fold strip, have them tell what number they have. Put those having the number two in pairs and those with the number one will be your singles.

➤ **Ask those who have #1 and are single for the purpose of this game,** how do they feel about being single. Ask the singles aren't they still human beings? Aren't they still loved by God? How should they feel about themselves, even though they aren't in a relationship?

➤ **Ask those in pairs, how do they feel about being in a relationship.** What does it do for them? Does God love them more because they are in a relationship? Are they better or more spiritual than those who are single because they are in a relationship?

GROWING TOGETHER (50 TO 60 MINUTES)

➤ **Constantly remind your disciples that God loves them no matter what!** They need to remember that they have God's DNA, thus, they have value, purpose and a destiny. They need to appreciate that they have self-worth, but aren't to worship themselves.

➤ **Single disciples should have a plan for the date before going on a date.** Listen carefully as disciples respond to the following questions about "Truth". Secular research consistently reveals that premarital sex is almost always the beginning of the end for most relationships.

➤ **It is critical to lay a foundation of your faith if you are going to practice 2 Corinthians 6:14-15.**

   ● **Why explain who you are on your first date (don't preach)?** If you become romantically involved with someone who doesn't share your beliefs, it will be difficult to end the relationship later because of your emotional attachment to that person, even if you know it needs to end.

- **This verse isn't saying that Christ followers are better than others.** To think that is to miss the point. The emphasis is not being unequally tied together. Once you get used to the other person's good looks and other things you like about that person, you will bond. What you believe is critical to who you are!

- **So asking if the person is a Christ follower on your first date is wise.** If your date says, "yes, he or she is a follower of Christ, then, ask him or her to tell you how he or she became one. You want to hear (1) what his or her life was life like before Christ; (2) what sparked his or her interest in Christ; (3) you need to hear that he or she asked Jesus Christ to forgive him or her for his or her sins and for Christ to come into his or her life; and (4) what his or her life has been since Christ as been in his or her life.

➤ **One of Dr. Gary Chapman's principles is Parental Consent.** You don't have to have your parents' consent, but if they love you whether they are Christ followers or not, they can tell who is and who isn't a good match for you. So don't easily dismiss their input.

➤ **It is wise having someone pray for you** as well as someone who has your best interest at heart when you might not be too objective due to your emotions.

CULTIVATING OUR SPIRIT (15 TO 20 MINUTES)
➤ Ask for your disciples to quote: Matthew 6:33; 2 Corinthians 6:14.

BEARING FRUIT (10 TO 15 MINUTES)
➤ Have your conversational prayer with disciples. Agree on a place to meet next week and adjourn.

Growing a Relationship That Lasts

➤ **Usual Opening**
➤ **Relationship sessions require prayer and sensitivity.** Divorce is prevalent in our culture, few are unaffected by it. Your disciples might be children of divorce or divorced themselves. It is essential they don't feel like second-class citizens during the discussion of this biblical institution of

marriage. Simultaneously, we must not be ashamed of teaching God's principles about marriage.

➤ **Tread lightly.** Some disciples may equate their self-worth to their relationship status. Some married couples may be struggling in their marriage.

➤ **If you have married couples, the Ground Rule is:** one spouse **cannot embarrass the other!** If a spouse desires to share something personal about the marriage, the other spouse must agree to share it.

HELPING HANDS (15-20 MINUTES)

➤ **Married couples must understand their fellowship with God is inextricably linked to their relationship with their spouse.** The phrase "fellowship with God" is being used here instead of relationship because a Christ follower's relationship is never in jeopardy because of eternal security (once a son or a daughter, always a son or daughter). Humans unfortunately can and do sever relationships. The critical point of emphasis is that the quality of the marriage reflects the quality of that individual's fellowship with God. A spouse won't experience all of God's Blessings if he or she isn't in a good relationship with his or her spouse.

➤ **Disciples also must understand that:** (1) God created marriage, so He has the best blueprint for it; (2) seldom is divorce the best solution for marital problems; (3) gain some tips for solving conflict; and (4) for your single disciples to have a better understanding about relationships. It doesn't have to be done in this order.

➤ **God Himself is a God of relationships.** There is God the Father, God the Son, and God the Holy Spirit.

GROWING TOGETHER (50 TO 60 MINUTES)

➤ **Since Paul was a Pharisee**, he was probably married and his wife left him or he granted her a divorce (1 Corinthians 7:12-15). Historical research reveals that marriage was a requirement for membership in the Sanhedrin. Paul says in Acts 23:6 and Philippians 3:5, that he is a Pharisee. In 1 Corinthians 7, Paul doesn't refer to himself as a virgin.

➤ **God understands being single. Jesus Christ never married.** He was a single. Encourage single disciples that being single isn't abnormal. Also encourage married couples not to make singles in their families, in this group or at church feel abnormal because they are single.

➤ God wants us to reflect His image in marriage, fulfillment and pleasure in the relationship, to enjoy having sex with each other, which should increase a couple's intimacy, monogamy, and to reproduce.

➤ **Philippians 2:1-5 emphasizes putting your spouse first after God!** It can revolutionize your marriage! Holding hands while praying together bond couples' spirits together.

➤ Dr. Phil says in his book, *Relationship Rescue*, "**this praying lowers a couples' divorce chances to one out of ten thousand!**" Praying is almost like having divorce insurance.

➤ A wife's responsibility is to submit. **Submit is a voluntary yielding, not a command. There is power in submission.** Christ submitted to His Father and Christ was rewarded for it! Submission doesn't keep the wife from having input in decisions. The husband's responsibility is to love his wife like himself. He is to initiate time in the Word with her. He is held responsible to God for her spiritual growth, but not her pastor. He is to be a servant leader, not a dictator! He is to put his wife's needs first! The wife is to put her husband's needs first. **The wife can turn the man's head, not by her words, but by her consistent godly behavior!**

➤ Anger isn't a sin, but can lead to sin. Refer disciples to the Building Lasting Relationships website, **Video Teachings** to view his teaching on conflict. Speaking the truth in love is not giving your spouse or anyone a piece of your mind. It is telling your spouse something he or she might not want to hear, but needs to hear. You tell your spouse at a time, in a tone, and way that he or she can receive (doesn't mean they will agree, but understand) what you are trying to communicate.

➤ **According to Luke 17:4 & Mark 11:25,** (just a few verses), God commands forgiveness. It isn't a feeling. **Forgiveness doesn't eliminate accountability or responsibility.** Revenge belongs to God according to Romans 12. Unforgiveness imprisons you! **View BLR's video on Biblical Forgiveness.** Recommend this video to your disciples. Encourage couples dating or married to grant or ask for forgiveness if it is needed in their relationships.

➤ **Sex is God's gift to married couples.** Sex isn't cheap, there is an investment each spouse must make in each other. Great marriages should have great sex! According to 1 Corinthians 7:1-5, Christian couples should have sex on a frequent basis! Every time you have sex with your spouse, you are renewing your Marriage Covenant with God, your spouse and yourself.

➤ **God created marriage to last a lifetime**. Divorce destroys what God loves. It is His first institution He created to bring pleasure to humans because He is a God of relationships. He knows what divorce does to couples and their children, who usually assume the divorce is there fault. God hates divorce, but He doesn't hate divorced people. God knows that when couples divorce, they usually marry and divorce again 2, 3 or 4 or more times. Every divorce lowers that person's ability to stay committed. And children grow up with no model of how to build a marriage to last a lifetime. *Psychology Today*, Feb. 6, 2012

➤ **Biblically, there are only two grounds for divorce**: adultery and desertion (1 Corinthians 7). Also in 1 Corinthians 7, God allows for separation. Tread gently here. Your goal isn't to argue, but restate God's teaching.

CULTIVATING OUR SPIRIT (15 TO 20 MINUTES)
➤ Have disciples quote memory verse: Ephesians 5:33

BEARING FRUIT (10 TO 15 MINUTES)
➤ **Have usual closing.**

PART 5: MODELING

Managing Money

➤ Have usual opening. How much money we have, how much money we make and how we spend our money can be the cause of celebration or depression.

➤ **Disciples need to know and embrace that God is the source of All!** God created everything and everyone! The money we have and/or make is really His! God even gives us the brains and physical skills to earn money.

HELPING HANDS (15-20 MINUTES)
➤ For this exercise, tell everyone to pretend they have just received a gift of $5,000. What will they do with it and why? Give each disciple 1-minute to explain what he or she would do with the money and why?

➤ Seldom do I give money to people on street corners on traffic islands by traffic lights. Once in a while, I do give cash to people on the streets asking for money. Typically, if I feel moved by the Holy Spirit to give, I will take that person for a meal. It isn't a sin to give or not give, unless the Holy Spirit tells you what to do and you disobey.

GROWING TOGETHER (50 TO 60 MINUTES)
➤ Few people are taught how to manage money or plan for the future financially.
➤ **God owns everything and created you.** So God is letting all of us be stewards of ourselves and the money He allows to cross our path.
➤ **God commands Christ followers to help the poor.** God knows it is giving and sharing that make us rich emotionally and fulfilled. We can't erase poverty. Jesus says the poor will always exists. But if we choose not to help those we can, we are the ones who are really poor! Proverbs 21:13; Proverbs 29:7 If we ignore the poor, God will ignore you when you need help. The godly care about the rights of the poor.
➤ **According to 1 Timothy 5:17-18**, those who are feeding you spiritually, should be supported by you financially. Some Old Testament tithes fed the priests, who worked only in the Temple or Tabernacle.
➤ **According to 1 Corinthians 16:1-2**, giving is an act of worship, so even if you get paid once a month, plan ahead so you can give part of your monthly giving to God as an act of worship.
➤ **A tithe is ten percent.** Israelites gave ten percent from the livestock, ten percent from produce and once every 3 years, a tenth of the harvest. So they tithed twenty and a half percent. If they borrowed against their tithe, which they could lawfully do, there was a twenty percent interest fee.
➤ **Don't give to be seen in public for the praise of people.**

CULTIVATING OUR SPIRIT (15 TO 20 MINUTES)
➤ Memory verses: 2 Corinthians 9:7–8. Before your group prays, share prayer requests. Include any updates to requests shared in previous sessions. Continue keeping some type of notebook record of how God is answering the prayers of your group.

BEARING FRUIT (10 TO 15 MINUTES)
➤ Field any questions your disciples may have. Have conversational prayer.

Be willing to meet with any individually during the upcoming week. Agree on a place to meet next week and adjourn.

Knowing Our Enemy

Before this session, it is critical to have people praying for your family, your disciples, their families, and you. Satan isn't going to sit quietly and allow you to educate followers of Christ about him. Don't be surprised, especially the week before this session, this week and the following weeks if things and people begin acting crazy around you, even other believers. Bathe yourself, your family and disciples in prayer.

➤ **Have usual opening.**

HELPING HANDS (15-20 MINUTES)
➤ Watch the group for those who appear uncomfortable. Hopefully, by now, the group has become a "Safe" place to share and a Sanctuary.
➤ During this section, keep an eye on the clock. See if anyone is being traumatized by thinking of a bully from their past.
➤ **Realize before you ask about bullies from their past**, that there is probably at least one or more disciples who have been abused emotionally and/or physically, be aware if everyone doesn't answer. Don't press this, but allow for sharing. Their sharing may take the entire time together, this is okay. **If someone shares their abuse, "Praise" them and "Thank" them for sharing.** Tell them you are sorry for what happened to them, but that every time they share—they are developing more closure and lessening the pain. And that their sharing may help others who are not where they are—in their ability to share their painful past.

GROWING TOGETHER (50 TO 60 MINUTES)
➤ **Your disciples really need your leadership and biblical authority for this session.** It is even possible for Satan to have planted a false disciple in your group for this session to cause confusion—so be very careful. No need to fear, but be careful.
➤ **This is a great time to have disciples quote 1 John 4:4.**
➤ **One of the purposes for memorizing so many verses is because the War**

Zone between God and Satan is for your mind. Jesus, when tempted by Satan in the wilderness, defeated Satan by quoting Bible verses.

➤ Satan wants to accuse and confuse us by deception. He wants to get our focus off of God and on ourselves and our circumstances.

➤ Satan is powerful, but he is not all-powerful. He has to get God's permission to do anything to us and God's other creations. His demons asked for permission to enter the pigs in Mark 5:1-13. God's very words are more powerful than Satan and his demons! So Satan has limited power.

➤ Satan's influence can be seen in the negative changes in our culture's morality (more profanity and nudity on regular TV), a fascination with violence (look at video games) an increase in hatred of others, the increase in killing worldwide, the increased emphasis in self (and your "Rights") and a lack of concern for our fellow humans-road rage. Human life in general has been devalued.

➤ Satan is extremely subtle! He uses a gradual plan of challenging God's values. For example, when the Ten Commandments were taken out of public school in the 1960's, there wasn't a major behavioral change in students because of the culture at that time. If a generation is approximately 20 years, look at the changes in two to almost three generations.

➤ We defeat Satan when we use God's way of escape mentioned in 1 Corinthians 10:13. Christ followers defeat Satan by using God's Word (memorizing it-we don't always have a Bible with us-I know most of us have cellphones), with prayer (individual & with others), putting on the spiritual armor mentioned in Ephesians 6:10-18, with faith, by extending grace to others (1 Corinthians 6:7—grace is implied)-this is supernatural-done with the Holy Spirit's power, by forgiving others, and with obedience.

➤ It is essential here, that your disciples know that God doesn't appear to send most of His disciples into head on encounters with Satan. Reassure them. But they do need to be aware of what tools they have.

CULTIVATING OUR SPIRIT (15 TO 20 MINUTES)

➤ Have disciples quote memory verses: 1 Peter 5:8–9; 1 John 4:4.

➤ Before praying within your group, you'll share prayer requests. Be sure to include any updates to requests you shared in the previous sessions. See if disciples are using prayer notebooks.

BEARING FRUIT (10 TO 15 MINUTES)

➤ Field any questions your disciples may have. Be willing to meet with any individually during the upcoming week. Do conversational prayer. You close in prayer to alleviate any fear and pray encouraging work. Agree on a place to meet next week and adjourn.

Using Technology

➤ **Have usual opening.**
➤ **Ask for a volunteer among your disciples** (if they have already prayed before at the close of a group session) to open this group time in a brief prayer for God's Blessings, for disciples and your time together. Don't ask someone who has never prayed in front of the group because this might embarrass him/her. Keep the personal touch—letting them experience your constant love and concern.
➤ **Ask the Holy Spirit for His wisdom as you lead this session.** Ask for Him to protect all of you from the evil one and for the Holy Spirit to have free reign in the session tonight and that God the Father will be glorified!
➤ **Your goal for this session is not to be for or against technology,** even if it is your strength or if you are technologically challenged. But for your disciples to biblically evaluate their use of technology and if they need to make any changes. Be careful not to have disciples taking sides on the pros or cons of technology because this isn't the issue. If this happens, stop and redirect the discussion. Explain why you are doing so.
➤ **This session may take longer to complete, so watch your time.** Try to finish on time, but don't make disciples feel rushed. Your disciples are always more important than finishing on time. But get permission from every one if you want to go beyond the usual ending time. If one person, says, "No," then, end on time, without that person feeling condemned. You want to complete each session every time you meet, but if the Holy Spirit guides you, you may need to divide a session into two.

HELPING HANDS (15-20 MINUTES)

➤ Everyone doesn't need to answer, only two or three. Watch the clock!
➤ **As questions are answered, remember not to let people take sides** or they will miss the point of this session. Help them think inclusively. The

issue isn't whether technology is good or bad, but as Christ followers are we using it to glorify God.

➤ **We've always had communication. Now, it is so much faster!** There is less privacy. Today, we can see a video of our favorite song performed by our favorite group. Many years ago, this wasn't possible unless you went to a concert or saw your favorite group on TV. Back in the heyday of radio, before videos, you heard a song and used the power of your imagination. Once you see a video that image and song are locked in your mind.

➤ **Emphasis here is not that technology is bad, but be aware of poor judgment in how it is sometimes used.** Also, people use social media to say things publicly that they would never say in person. Such action is a form of abuse. In some cases, could be bullying. Additionally, even in relationships, people often communicate emotional issues that should demand a face-to-face conservation, but don't. Face-to-face provides body language, eye contact, tone, and voice inflection. All of these factors are crucial to honest communication. Without these factors, communication can easily be and often is miscommunicated.

➤ **Being afraid to confront someone face-to-face and choosing to do so via social media is a cop-out and reflects our character and integrity.** Sure face-to-face is uncomfortable, but this is when our faith should remind us that we are to glorify God in all our actions.

GROWING TOGETHER (50 TO 60 MINUTES)

➤ **In 1 Timothy 3:4-5, don't focus on the husband being the head of the house.** Focus on managing the household well. Could that include managing time with loved ones? Even though most of us will spend more time at work, our priority should be our loved ones. The issue isn't about balancing family and work because to balance them means you are giving them equal value. We need to focus on managing family and work, with work only as a way to support our family. Thus, we need to discuss with loved ones how to maximize our times together. Ephesians 5:21 might help here.

➤ **If you're not sure about communicating a particular message via social media**, then, don't! Romans 14:22-23. Galatians 5:22-23-one of the Fruit of the Spirit is peace. Have peace from God about your social media communication.

CULTIVATING OUR SPIRIT (15 TO 20 MINUTES)
➤ Have disciples quote memory verses: Colossians 1:16; 3:23–24
➤ Be sure to include any updates to requests you shared in the previous sessions. Consider how God is answering the prayers of your group.

BEARING FRUIT (10 TO 15 MINUTES)
➤ The disciples and you should be keeping a Prayer Notebook by now to record how God is answering the prayers of your group. Have usual closing including conversational prayer.

Fearing and Faith

➤ **Have usual opening.**
➤ **Most of us have been afraid of something at some point in time in our lives.** There is no shame in that. But we should not have an ongoing fear of anything as a Christ follower.
➤ **This is another vulnerability session.** Each session should result in more intimacy and trust for your disciples and you with each other.
➤ As always, observe how disciples are emotionally handling this session.

HELPING HANDS (15-20 MINUTES)
➤ **It is common for our fear to be passed on to those we influence.** Typically, fear can paralyze us, keeping us from thinking clearly. It can keep us from seeing the big picture and it can keep us from initially going to God for help. Thus, fear can affect our faith.
➤ **Don't be surprised by what causes fear in a person.** It is critical that you shower your disciples with God's love. They must feel secure and safe with this group and you. They may not share, but the key is them hearing and experiencing God's love for them in this session.

GROWING TOGETHER (50 TO 60 MINUTES)
➤ **Listen carefully to your disciples as they share their fears. Don't force anyone to tell his or her fear.** After some have shared their fears and defined fear, remind them of Joshua, who was Moses' assistant. Ask a disciple to read Joshua 1:6-9 &18. Ask the group, "Joshua saw miracles with Moses! Why do you think God told Joshua three times to be strong and

courageous?" Was Joshua hard of hearing? **Possible answer:** Joshua was probably insecure about himself and the incredible task before him. He was not the bold personality that Moses was.

➤ *"As a inquisitive young boy, who believed rules were made to be broken, I often found myself worried if my disobedience to Mom would be severe enough to cause Dad to spank me. Dad could inflict serious pain! Often, I regretted making bad decisions."* —Clarence

➤ **God is our source and strength to help all of us overcome our fear.** It isn't a shame or sinful to have fear. But we don't need to let fear dominate us or prevent us from being free from our fearful thoughts controlling us.

➤ **This is an excellent place to have your disciples quote 2 Timothy 1:7.** By now, all disciples should be quoting their verses. They should know all the verses. Periodically as for memory verses from other sessions that are appropriate for current session.

CULTIVATING OUR SPIRIT (15 TO 20 MINUTES)
➤ Have disciples quote Memory verses: Joshua 1:8–9; 2 Timothy 1:7

BEARING FRUIT (10 TO 15 MINUTES)
➤ See how God is answering the prayers of your group. Continue urging disciples to use their prayer notebooks. Have your conversational prayer with disciples. Agree on a place to meet next week and adjourn.

Fulfilled and Fruitful

➤ **Have usual opening.**
➤ **Congratulate your disciple candidates on completing this discipleship course!** It is a lot of work! For this last session, you may want to have a special dinner before beginning the session or a dessert time after this session.
➤ **At this dinner or dessert, individually praise each disciple candidate for his or her commitment.** Share about each disciple candidate's uniqueness or giftedness. Share what you learned from each disciple if possible. If you have time the week of this session or weeks before, give a handwritten note of encouragement and appreciation. This will save time of addressing each disciple during the session. It is up to you.

➤ **Tell them if you are doing a dinner or a dessert, that this session will probably be 2 ½ hours long.** You determine the length of your celebration. Or you could have a special time the following week.

➤ **Your goal after the celebration is one last challenge for your disciple candidates to become disciples by spiritually making new disciples.**

➤ **Ask disciples if they have graduated from anything.** It could be elementary school or anything. Ask them how it felt to graduate. **You want to know if graduating gave them hope.** Ask them, "What is the purpose of graduating from anything? **Graduation should prepare you for a task or purpose.** What is the point of graduating, but not doing what you were prepared to do? How would you feel?

➤ **This time is a review of all they have learned.** The sessions are their quiz. Ask them to answer questions from memory. Memory verses are fair game. The purpose of the questions isn't to embarrass, but to help them see what they have learned.

➤ **Please don't be limited by my suggested questions.** Feel free to use your own.

➤ During this time, you want to hear from each disciple candidate. This is a time for you to listen, learn, evaluate and be Blessed by your disciple candidates. They are disciple candidates until they produce a disciple.

➤ Have your disciple candidates turn back to specific questions in the sessions for this group time and ask them questions. Let each disciple, if possible, respond to the questions below.

➤ **Have your disciples close this final session in prayer.**

➤ **During the following week, contact those disciples you feel are ready to being discipling others.** Encourage them to take a 2-3 week break and then start their own discipleship group so they can give you spiritual grandbabies!

Congratulations to you for leading your disciples through this workbook! I'm so proud of you and blessed by you!

Marriage Resources

Five Love Languages, Dr. Gary Chapman, Moody Publishing.

Keeping Your Wife Your Best Friend, Dr. Clarence Shuler, BLR: Building Lasting Relationships Publishing (available through Dr. Shuler's website: www. clarenceshuler.com, click on bookstore).

Seven Rings of Marriage, Jackie and Stephana Bledsoe, LifeWay.

Intimacy Ignited: Fire Up Your Sex Life with the Song of Solomon, Dr. Joseph and Linda Dillow and Dr. Peter and Lorraine Pintus, NAVPRESS.

Languages of Apology, Dr. Gary Chapman and Dr. Jennifer Thomas, Moody Publishing.

Love Is A Verb: Stories of What Happens When Love Comes Alive, Dr. Gary Chapman, Bethany House.

The Love Dare (from the movie Fireproof), Stephen and Alex Kendrick with Lawrence Kimbrough, B &H Publishing Group.

The Dance of Restoration: Rebuilding Marriage After Infidelity, Abel Ortega and Melodie Fleming, Living Ink Books.

Prayer Journal

More Down-to-Earth Insights from
Dr. Clarence Shuler

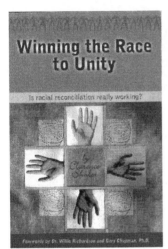

Winning the Race to Unity
ISBN- 10: 0-8024-8159-0

Winning the Race to Unity is thorough, insightful, provocative, and distinctly Christian. Clarence Shuler has given us an excellent resource to stimulate, guide and stretch us in our interracial relationships, so we as Christ's followers can lead the way instead of always trying to catch up. This book is to be read, discussed, prayed over and acted upon. I highly recommend it.
—RANDY ALCORN, author of *Heaven* and *The Purity Principle*

What All Dads Should Know
with Dr. Jeffrey Shears
ISBN: 978-146622553-4

It is not difficult to be a biological father, but it is extremely difficult to be a successful father. All of us had fathers; some good, some great, some absent, and some abusive. I've never met a man who wanted to be a bad father. Most of us would like to be loving, kind, supportive, and good role models for our children. But most of us need help to make that desire a reality. In *What All Dads Should Know,* Drs. Shears and Shuler offer such help. The book is readable and practical. I highly recommend it to all fathers.
—GARY CHAPMAN, Ph.D., Author of *The Five Love Languages*

Your Wife Can Be Your Best Friend
ISBN: 9781470020170

In these pages, Clarence engages our minds and hearts... he shows us how to nurture the relationship with our life partner and identifies what it will take for her to be our best friend. This book is a valuable resource and a treasured tool to move us from self-centeredness to self-sacrifice.
—DR. CRAWFORD LORITTS, JR., Senior Pastor Fellowship Bible Church

Single and Free to Be Me
with Myrna Gutierrez
ISBN- 13: 978-1480280038

Want to get off the exhausting treadmill of feeling you have to be in a relationship? Are you confused about how to be a Christian single in today's changing culture? *Single and Free to Be Me* enables singles regardless of age or gender to: (1) Focus on their true identity whether they are in a relationship or not; (2) Free them from the pressures the church and society put on them; (3) Help heal singles wounded by previous relationships; and (4) Provides a self-evaluation checklist educating singles as to whether they are healthy and ready for a new relationship, including marriage. Excellent source for singles ministry leaders.

All titles are available on Kindle and at www.clarenceshuler.com.

Speaking Engagements

To Book Clarence Shuler for Speaking Engagements: Call 719-282-1340 or Email him at Clarence.BLR@gmail.com

Women love his *Understanding the Heart of A Man* seminar!
Millennials find his *Pursuing Holiness & Purity in a Pornographic Age* refreshing!

Made in the USA
Columbia, SC
29 December 2018